WALTER KERN

NEW LITURGY
and
OLD DEVOTIONS

EXPLANATIONS AND PRAYERS

D1457707

ALBA BOOKS

DEDICATION
TO
MY FAMILY AND RELATIVES

Nihil Obstat:

Rev. Ralph Miller

Imprimatur:

+ Edward D. Head, D.D.
Bishop of Buffalo

June 2, 1978

Library of Congress Catalog Card No. 78-73623

ISBN 0-8189-1151-4

© Copyright, 1979, Alba House Communications

Canfield, Ohio 44406

Printed in the United States of America

CONTENTS

*Rejoice in the Lord always! I say it again.
Rejoice! Everyone should see how unselfish you are.
The Lord is near. Present your needs to God in every
form of prayer and in petitions full of gratitude. Then
God's peace, which is beyond all understanding, will stand
guard over your hearts and minds, in Christ Jesus.*
(Philippians 4:4-9)

ACKNOWLEDGEMENTS

Photographs by Gerald Mangan, Niagara Falls, N.Y.

Bible quotations from the *New American Bible,* © 1970, used herein by permission of the Confraternity of Christian Doctrine, Washington, D. C.

English translations of prayers, litany of the saints, and quotations from the *Roman Missal,* © 1973, and *Holy Communion and Worship of the Eucharist Outside of Mass,* © 1974, by International Committee on English in the Liturgy, Inc. All rights reserved.

Quotations from *Instruction on Eucharistic Worship,* © 1967, *Behold Your Mother,* © 1973, and *Marian Devotions,* © 1974, used herein by permission of the Publications Office of the United States Catholic Conference, Washington, D. C.

Prayers from The *Maryknoll Missal,* © 1966, used herein with permission of P. J. Kennedy & Sons, New York, N. Y.

1

LITURGICAL
PIETY

Recently I came across some old notebooks in which former parish priests wrote out the announcements to be read at Mass. The earliest is for the year 1930. As I read them, I was amazed to note how rich the prayer-life of the average American parish was beyond the Mass and Sacraments.

There was the liturgical procession in connection with the blessing of candles on February 2; the blessing of throats in honor of St. Blaise on February 3; the Ember Days in Spring, Summer, Autumn, and Winter for blessings on agriculture and for priests; a triduum in honor of St. Joseph in March; the Lenten devotions on Wednesday (sermon and Benediction), Friday Stations and Benediction, Sunday evening devotions and Benediction.

There was a liturgical litany and procession in honor of St. Mark for good crops; May devotions and Benediction every evening, with a May crowning at the end of the month; three days of eucharistic devotions called Forty Hours—as a highpoint

of parish eucharistic devotions; the charming ceremonies for First Communion; a Pentecost novena;
a Corpus Christi procession with Benediction at
two outdoor altars and another back in the church;
a June novena to the Sacred Heart; Rosary devotions during October; a Christmas novena, and so
on.

Each week there was a Sunday evening devotion with Benediction; a Tuesday novena alternately
in honor of St. Anthony and St. Theresa; and a Wednesday novena in honor of Our Lady of the Miraculous Medal. Finally, every First Friday, besides
the usual Mass and extra distribution of Communion
in reparation for sin, there was exposition of the
Blessed Sacrament all day, with devotions and
Benediction in the evening. A Holy Hour was announced as a "new" practice to be inaugurated in
the parish for every Friday evening at 8:00 P.M.

One has to admire the sheer quantity of the
services which the ordinary parish priest offered
to his community, besides the Mass, Sacraments,
and Sacramentals. One also has to recognize the
piety of the average parishioner, who often came
at least one evening as an "extra" besides his or her
weekly attendance at Mass. And, finally, one has
to say a good word for the communal nature of so
many of these services, which drew priest and
people together at their Father's House in prayer
and heart-felt song.

While people did attend Mass and receive the
Sacraments with regularity, I imagine it would not
be incorrect to say that the warm part of their

religious life did not center on the official, public worship of the Church (the Mass, the Sacraments, the Divine Office—now called the Liturgy of the Hours—the Liturgical Year, and the Scriptures), but rather on this wide variety of prayers and devotions. These many practices were all carefully and personally selected to suit each one's spiritual sensitivity and education. They were used not only in these non-liturgical services at church—and often during the "quiet parts" of the Latin Mass itself—but were also adapted for use at home and in connection with church society meetings.

In view of all this, one might ask why many of these devotions have either disappeared or gone underground in the decade since the issuing of the II Vatican Council's great document on worship, "The Constitution on the Sacred Liturgy"? The following chapters will explore what the II Vatican Council and its post-conciliar commissions had to say about the liturgy and the relationship of this devotional prayer to the liturgy. They will ask whether popular devotions have any relevance in the contemporary Church or not. Finally, if some merit can be found for such devotional prayer, one must further inquire what can be done to update them.

WHAT ARE POPULAR DEVOTIONS?

All forms of prayer are basically "conversation with God"—as St. Clement of Alexandria wrote in the 2nd Century. "Prayer, ah, prayer," wrote St.

Elizabeth Seton, "Our speaking with God, our infinite beloved."

Sometimes this dialogue takes on the form of a wordless conversation between persons; at other times it is the rambling, free form of talk of people who appreciate each other so that form is not important; on still other occasions one prays with carefully composed formulas to say fully and well what one wishes to convey to God; and, finally, prayer can be in the lofty form of the liturgy. Each form of prayer can lead the soul to union with God, as well as attune the individual to listen to God—the other direction of prayer activities.

Prayer usually takes on one or more of the classical expressions of dialogue with God: adoration, praise, thanksgiving, reparation, and petition.

Adoration is acknowledgment of the unique nature and greatness of God, with admission of our absolute dependence on him.

Praise is joyful recognition of God's greatness and goodness to all.

Thanksgiving is gratitude for all of God's gifts and blessings both to ourselves and to all mankind.

Reparation is owning up to our unfaithful love, with suitable sorrow and efforts to improve.

Petition is admission of our need of God, source of all goodness, with confident requests made because he urges us to do so.

Love has not been included as one of these basic expressions of prayer because love is or should be involved in all of them. One should offer God loving-adoration, loving-praise, loving-thanksgiving, loving-sorrow, and loving-petition.

If we recognize that these prayer expressions should be found in all forms of prayer, then we can go on to see that they are part of all good liturgical prayer and, of all good non-liturgical prayer. The whole question of liturgical prayer and the non-liturgical prayer (to which devotions pertain) is that of the relationship of the one to the other.

Some pre-conciliar liturgists wrote that pre-conciliar piety was a devotional piety, whereas it should have been a liturgical piety. What is the difference?

Devotional prayer can be described as prayer forms often joined with readings, song, symbol and ceremony aimed at nourishing the worship needs of the faithful outside of the liturgy, but preparing them for it and trying to make it more effective in their everyday life. Devotional prayer has been called, at one time or another, "non-liturgical," "extra-liturgical," and "paraliturgical" prayer. More recent writings prefer the word, paraliturgical, for devotional prayer, but some writers seem to use that word to designate group celebrations of devotional prayer.

There are three types of non-liturgical or paraliturgical prayer.

First, there are those prayer activities under the direct supervision of the local bishop, which he sometimes commits to a diocesan prayer book. Josef Jungmann, the great liturgist, suggested that they might be called "diocesan liturgy". The II Vatican Council designated them "devotions proper to the individual churches" or "sacra exercitia", in the *Constitution on the Sacred Liturgy*, n. 13.

In practice, few bishops seem to issue such diocesan prayer books. Perhaps, this designation should be applied to all the cathedral ceremonies which the bishop supervises, either personally or through his diocesan liturgical commission, and issues in some printed form *as models* for his diocese. This would pertain to all prayer and religious services in addition to Mass, the Sacraments, and the Liturgy of the Hours.

Second, there are prayer activities used at gatherings of the faithful, usually with a priest or deacon. The II Vatican Council termed them "popular devotions of the Christian peoples" or "pia exercitia" —also in n. 13 in the Constitution. Some examples might be the Rosary, the Way of the Cross and shared or Charismatic prayer meetings.

Finally, there are all the prayers *and* above-mentioned activities which an individual might use alone or within the privacy of the circle of his family and friends. In actual practice, the first two types often blend into one: we can simply speak of popular devotions and private prayer.

The *Constitution on the Sacred Liturgy* refers to the fact that there is more to our prayer life than the liturgy, "the source and summit." In n. 9 we read: "The sacred liturgy does not exhaust the entire activity of the Church. Before men can come to the liturgy, they must be called to faith and conversion."

Again in n. 12 we read: "The spiritual life, however, is not confined to participation in the liturgy. The Christian is assuredly called to pray with his brethren, but he must also enter into his chamber to pray to the Father in secret; indeed, according to the Apostle Paul, he should pray without ceasing." Then the Constitution goes on to discuss in n. 13 the Council's teaching on popular devotions.

In other documents of the same Council, we find great insistence on prayer. The *Dogmatic Constitution on the Church* addresses itself to the prayer of the laity, especially the married (n. 34). Family prayer is discussed in the *Pastoral Constitution on the Church in the Modern World* (n. 34). The prayer life of the priest is considered in the *Decree on the Ministry and Life of the Priest* (n. 18). The prayer of the religious is taken into consideration in the *Decree on Appropriate Renewal of Religious Life* (n. 6). These references, naturally, are not the only ones of the Council on prayer, but they are very representative.

WHAT IS THE VALUE OF DEVOTIONAL PRAYER?

Popular devotions and private prayer should always be seen in relationship to the liturgy. They help the liturgy (which is the superior prayer) be more effective in our everyday world. They usually remind us of one or more of the great truths of our faith, invite our work-a-day commitment to these truths, bring us back into the presence of God amid our daily activities, encourage us as we work out our difficulties, and aid us to grow in love and service of God and neighbor.

There is no true opposition between authentic private prayer and devotions and authentic liturgy. The liturgy presupposes the presence of other forms of prayer and depends upon them. While it is true that some devotional prayer did develop during periods when the liturgy was at a low, much of it grew under the inspiration of the Holy Spirit alongside of the liturgy. The liturgy should not reject devotions, but rather permeate and guide them with its spirit and norms, and use them as auxiliaries and helpmates. (The liturgy has some moments for silent personal prayer, but non-liturgical devotions should not be used by people during Mass. Cfr. *Marian Devotions.* n. 48.)

In describing devotional prayer, one must be careful not to center this concept only on *written* formulas of prayer. One can say prayers without deeply engaging the heart or mind, but it is only when the heart and mind have been united with God that real prayer takes place. (It's the difference between praying and "prayers." Prayers are only a means to this praying or conversation with God.)

When speaking of such prayer, it is presupposed that we do not use only prayer formulas in our conversation with God. We should engage in meditation on a regular and serious basis, as well as in other forms of prayer.

With this general description of devotions in mind, as well as their value in our spiritual life, we are now ready to go on to ask what is liturgical piety?

WHAT IS LITURGICAL PIETY?

Perhaps a good way to begin a description of liturgical piety is to use an image describing such a Christian life. The Christian life can be likened to a *spiral* in which the Christian gains grace and strength from the liturgy to go out to love and be of service to God and neighbor, then comes back to the liturgy with the gifts of that love and service to be offered to the Father in the Mass through the mediation of Christ in the Spirit. With the grace and strength of the Risen Christ, the Christian would again go out to love and serve God and neighbor even better.

All during life this spiral would grow and ascend. Into it private prayers and devotions would fit as means to aid the liturgy to achieve its purpose in daily life (between liturgies) as well as to prepare the Christian for a more meaningful celebration when he or she is again part of the liturgy. As spiral follows spiral, the final thrust would be into the Father's presence for the celebration of his love and goodness which goes on forever.

As the Council teaches, "Nevertheless, the liturgy is the summit toward which the activity of the Church is directed; at the same time it is the fountain from which all her power flows. For the goal of apostolic works is that all who are made sons of God by faith and baptism should come together to praise God in the midst of His Church, to take part in her sacrifice, and to eat the Lord's supper ....

From the liturgy, therefore, and especially from the Eucharist, as from a fountain, grace is chan-

19

neled into us; and the sanctification of men in Christ and the glorification of God, to which all other activities of the Church are directed as toward their goal, are most powerfully achieved" (*Constitution on the Sacred Liturgy*, n. 10).

Liturgical piety gains its power from the reality that Christ is present in his Church and uniquely joins the life and activities of all his members to himself especially in the liturgy, and offers them, with his prayer and activities, to the heavenly Father. The liturgy is the prayer and activity of the whole Christ, the Head and all the members, praying "through him, and with him, and in him" in the Spirit to our loving Father in heaven.

"Christ indeed always associates the Church with Himself in the great work of giving perfect praise to God and making men holy," writes the Council. "The Church is His dearly beloved Bride who calls to her Lord, and through Him offers worship to the Eternal Father. Rightly, then, the liturgy is considered as an exercise of the priestly office of Jesus Christ.

In the liturgy the sanctification of man is manifested in signs perceptible to the senses, and is effected in a way which is proper to each of these signs; in the liturgy full public worship is performed by the Mystical Body of Jesus Christ, that is, by the Head and His members. From this it follows that every liturgical celebration, because it is an action of Christ the priest and of His Body the Church, is a sacred action surpassing all others. No other action of the Church can match its claim to efficacy, nor equal the degree of it" *(Constitution on the Sacred Liturgy,* n. 7).

In practice, though, what are *some of the characteristics of such liturgical piety,* which the Council urges so strongly? There are many ways of describing it, but it has at least these six characteristics.

1. *Liturgical piety is rooted in the dynamic presence of the Risen Christ in his Church.*

In the great mystery of God's love affair with mankind, one must be ever aware of Christ as mediator of this relationship in the New Covenant. But it is the Risen Christ who is that mediator, glorified and ever present with his people! Not only is he present in the Eucharist in a "most unique way"; he is also present in his word, in the person of the priest, in the sacraments in which he truly acts, in the Church when it prays and sings, "where two or three are gathered in his name", in the hearts of all in his love and grace, in those who aid the least of the brethren and in those who are aided.

The *Constitution on the Sacred Liturgy* (n. 7) does not relate all these presences to each other, but they are true. An important task of the Christian at prayer and in life is to be united to the Risen Lord, and with his power and love, to be his willing partner in serving the brothers and sisters.

2. *Liturgical piety is rooted in the mystery of the Church.*

God, through his Son, loves all men and women, but not as isolated individuals. He wills to gather his people into his Church. When Christ prays with his people in the liturgy, that prayer has a power which the individual or any gathering of individuals can never achieve outside of the liturgy.

The Church is a mystery. She is God's sheepfold, his flock, field, vine, spiritual temple, holy city, virgin bride. All these biblical images—and the reality for which they stand—are outlined with others in the sixth and seventh sections of the *Dogmatic Constitution on the Church.*

Liturgical piety is a *communal, ecclesial* piety. There is certainly room in it for private and other forms of prayer; in fact, they are quite needed, but the "source and summit" is liturgical, communal prayer. "No other action of the Church can match its claim of efficacy, nor equal the degree of it" (n. 7).

Since it is really the prayer of Christ, Head and members, "Liturgical services are not private functions, but are celebrations of the Church, which is the sacrament of unity" (n. 26). "Such participation by the Christian people as a 'chosen race, a royal priesthood, a holy nation, a redeemed people' is their right and duty by reason of their baptism" (n. 14).

3. *Liturgical piety is rooted and nourished in the Sacred Scriptures.*

While private prayers and devotions are also influenced by the Bible, "Sacred Scripture is of paramount importance in the celebration of the liturgy. For it is from the Scripture that lessons are read and explained in the homily, and psalms are sung; the prayers, collects, and liturgical songs are scriptural in their inspiration, and it is from the Scripture that actions and signs derive their meaning. Thus if the restoration, progress, and adaptation of the sacred liturgy are to be achieved, it is necessary to promote that warm and living love for Scripture to which the venerable tradition of both Eastern and Western rites gives testimony" (n. 24).

Through the Scriptures God speaks to people and Christ is still proclaiming the Gospel (n. 7). All forms of prayer should be inspired by Scripture, and "the treasures of the Bible are to be opened more lavishly, so that richer fare be provided for the faithful at the table of God's word" (n. 51).

4. *Liturgical piety is centered on the essentials of the Church's public worship: on the eucharistic celebration, the sacraments, and the Liturgy of the Hours.*

In the Constitution we read: "For the liturgy, through which the work of our redemption is accomplished, most of all in the divine *sacrifice of the Eucharist,* is the outstanding means whereby the faithful may express in their lives, and manifest to others, the mystery of Christ and the real nature of the Church" (n. 6).

"The purpose of *the sacraments* is to sanctify men, to build up the body of Christ, and, finally, to give

23

worship to God; because they are signs they also instruct. They not only presuppose faith, but by words and objects they also nourish, strengthen, and express it; that is why they are called *"sacraments of faith"* .... It is therefore of the highest importance that the faithful should easily understand the sacramental signs and should frequent with greater eagerness those sacraments which were instituted to nourish the Christian life" (n. 59).

Finally, *the Liturgy of the Hours*—that prayer-form made up of psalms, hymns, readings, and prayers designed to be offered to sanctify the passage of time—is important. "By traditions going back to the early Christian times, the divine office is devised so that the whole course of the day and night is made holy by the praise of God ... Pastors of souls should see to it that the chief hours, especially Vespers, are celebrated in common in church on Sundays and more solemn feasts. And the laity, too, are encouraged to recite the divine office, either with priests, or among themselves, or even individually" (n. 84, 100).

In sum, the Church sees the Mass, the sacraments, and the Hours as the superior and more important prayer, because they are the prayer of the whole Church joined to her Head. Other prayers, important as they are, should always exist in relationship to these various forms of the official public worship of the Church.

5. *Liturgical piety follows the exposition of the mysteries of Christ through the Liturgical Year.*

"Holy Mother Church is conscious that she must

celebrate the saving works of her divine Spouse by devoutly recalling it on certain days throughout the course of the year ... within the cycle of a year, moreover, she unfolds the whole mystery of Christ, from the incarnation and birth until the ascension, but also as reflected in the days of Pentecost, and the expectation of a blessed, hoped-for return of the Lord. Recalling thus the mysteries of redemption, the Church opens to the faithful the riches of the Lord's powers and merits, so that these are in some way made present at all times and the faithful are enabled to lay hold of them and become filled with saving grace" (n. 102).

"The doctrine, that there is an obligation incumbent on all to conform to a spirituality that is liturgical," writes Constance Koser—in his lengthy and extremely thorough Chapter Eight on devotions in *"The Liturgy of Vatican II, A Symposium in Two Volumes"* (Franciscan Herald Press, Chicago, 1966) —"and to build up a spiritual life in accordance with it, must be recognized and duly respected. But it is important, too, to keep in mind that the Constitution expressly teaches that liturgy does not enjoy a monopoly in the spiritual life; on the contrary, it needs to be supplemented. Pious exercises are part of this supplementary aid that is needed, and so are other ecclesial exercises. These exercises must be built up in accordance with the liturgy, stem from it, and lead souls to it—but they still remain 'pious exercises' " (pp. 255-256).

WHAT ARE THE WORDS
OF THE COUNCIL ON DEVOTIONS?

With an idea in mind of what liturgical piety is like, one can now ask how the Council itself related devotions to the liturgy. The key section is the thirteenth one:

> "Popular devotions of the Christian people are warmly commended, provided they accord with the laws and norms of the Church. Such is especially the case with devotions called for by the Apostolic See.
>
> "Devotions proper to the individual churches also have a special dignity if they are conducted by mandate of the bishops in accord with customs or books lawfully approved.
>
> "Nevertheless those devotions should be drawn up that they harmonize with the liturgical seasons, accord with the sacred liturgy, are in some fashion derived from it, and lead the people to it, since the liturgy by its very nature far surpasses any of them." (*Constitution on the Sacred Liturgy*, n. 13.)

The Council does not condemn, suppress, or ignore popular devotions, but recognizes and warmly commends them, under certain conditions. After distinguishing between "liturgical" and "non-liturgical" piety, it asserts the superiority of the former and admits the usefulness of the latter. This will be the direction of the following chapters.

Each chapter will consider one or more of the better-known popular devotions, discuss its *history*, seek its *enduring value,* and offer some of many possible *suggestions for renewal.* A *Prayer Section* will follow each chapter to offer all the prayers needed to practice the devotion under consideration. Scriptural readings suitable for public devotional or paraliturgical services will be offered. Traditional and contemporary prayers will be given, in addition to a sampling of the rich Eastern Catholic prayer traditions. A general collection of prayers will be found at the end of the last chapter of this book.

SEASONAL LITURGICAL PRAYERS

A practical way to carry out the directive of the *Constitution on the Sacred Liturgy* to harmonize all popular devotions with the Liturgical Year is to add one of the following prayers to one's devotional prayers. They will also serve as models of well-written prayers when composing new ones. These prayers are taken from the Sacramentary. Many others, especially the Sunday Opening Prayer, can be found in the Missalette and the new hand missals.

1. *ADVENT SEASON.*

Lord God,
may we, your people,
who look forward to the birthday
  of Christ,
experience the joy of salvation
and celebrate that feast with love

and thanksgiving.
We ask this through Christ our Lord.

(Third Sunday of Advent.)

2. CHRISTMAS SEASON.

Father in heaven, creator of all,
you ordered the earth to bring forth life
and crowned its goodness by creating the
  family of man.
In history's moment when all was ready,
you sent your Son to dwell in time,
obedient to the laws of life in our world.
Teach us the sanctity of human love,
show us the value of family life,
and help us to live in peace with all men
that we may share in your life for ever.
We ask this through Christ our Lord.

(Feast of the Holy Family.)

3. EPIPHANY.

Father of light, unchanging God,
today you reveal to men of faith
the resplendent fact of the Word made
  flesh.
Your light is strong,
your love is near;
draw us beyond the limits which this
  world imposes,
to the life where your Spirit makes all

life complete.
We ask this through Christ our Lord.

(Solemnity of the Epiphany.)

4. *LENTEN SEASON.*

God of all compassion, Father of all
goodness,
to heal the wounds our sins and
selfishness bring upon us
you bid us turn to fasting, prayer, and
sharing with our brothers.
We acknowledge our sinfulness, our guilt
is ever before us:
when our weakness causes
discouragement,
let your compassion fill us with hope
and lead us through a Lent of repentance
to the beauty of Easter joy.
Grant this through Christ our Lord.

(Third Sunday of Lent.)

5. *HOLY WEEK.*

Lord,
by the suffering of Christ your Son
you have saved us all from the death
we inherited from sinful Adam.
By the law of nature
we have borne the likeness to his man-
hood.

30

May the sanctifying power of grace
help us put on the likeness of our
  Lord in heaven,
who lives and reigns for ever and ever.

  (Good Friday.)

6. *EASTER SEASON.*

God of mercy,
you wash away our sins in water,
you give us new birth in the Spirit,
and redeem us in the blood of Christ.
As we celebrate Christ's resurrection
increase our awareness of these
  blessings,
and renew your gift of life within us.
We ask this through Christ our Lord.

  (Second Sunday of Easter.)

7. *PENTECOST.*

Almighty and ever-living God,
you fulfill the Easter promise
by sending us your Holy Spirit.
May that Spirit unite the races and
  nations on earth
to proclaim your glory.
Grant this through Christ our Lord.

  (Vigil of Pentecost.)

8. *ANY SEASON.*

Father,
your love never fails.
Keep us from danger
and provide for all our needs.
Grant this through Christ our Lord.

(Ninth Sunday in Ordinary Time.)

9. *ANY SEASON.*

God our Father and protector,
without you nothing is holy,
nothing has value.
Guide us to everlasting life
by helping us to use wisely
the blessings you have given to
  the world.
We ask this through Christ our Lord.

(Seventeenth Sunday in Ordinary Time.)

10. *ANY SEASON.*

God our Father,
may we love you in all things and
  above all things
and reach the joy you have prepared
  for us
beyond all our imagining.
We ask this through Christ our Lord.

(Twentieth Sunday in Ordinary Time.)

2

RENEWING
POPULAR
DEVOTIONS

Some time ago, at a diocesan liturgical commission meeting, a member related an experience with a priest, who conducted one of the best known and better attended novena services in the city. The member said that he had suggested that even this fine devotion could be improved by applying the principles of Section 13 from the "Constitution on the Sacred Liturgy" to it.

"Why should I?", was the reply. "I've got a good thing going here, and why should I upset the applecart?" Perhaps this priest, and so many others, fail to understand their full role in the area of community and personal prayer. They are not mere leaders of prayer services, but also formers of their people's attitudes and guides in their growth in prayer.

HOW DEVOTIONAL PRAYER AROSE?

There is an impression among some liturgists that popular devotions and other paraliturgical prayer arose during periods of poor liturgical understanding and practice. The by-product of such a misconception is the idea that non-liturgical prayer beyond private prayer will disappear as soon as the liturgy is properly understood and used.

This attitude may be grounded in a reaction to the deficiencies of some particular popular devotion, a very uninformed use of such a devotion, or the memory of the way some individual close at hand may have practiced a certain devotion. If one sets aside that reaction for a moment and looks at Church history, a different attitude may be appropriate.

In the early days of the Church, there seems to have been no distinction between liturgy and non-liturgical prayer: there was simply prayer. Under the influence of the Holy Spirit, Christian hymns were written and used. Some of them were included by the inspired writers in the pages of the New Testament—for example, Philippians 2, 5-11. Later, under the influence of the Spirit, the Fathers of the Church were such prolific writers of songs and hymns that some of their works were introduced into the liturgies of the East and the West.

During the Middle Ages, numerous prayers, hymns, sequences, processions and religious folk customs were produced—and again, some found their way into the liturgy. Only in recent times were afternoon and evening devotions and services made available to the people in Latin or in the vernacular.

In America, non-English speaking people introduced Vespers, followed by Benediction. In English-
speaking parishes and institutions, one most frequently found the rosary with Benediction. (Since
Benediction followed Vespers, and the rosary service probably owes its origin to the prayers which
followed the Marian hymn, "Salve Regina", after
Compline, one can observe some influence of the
liturgy on these devotions.) While one must recognize some competition between a warm paraliturgical service and a poorly understood and poorly
participated Mass, this competition is not intrinsic.

It would be much closer to the facts of history
to see that the Holy Spirit has always been at
work in the Church inspiring people to provide
for the spiritual needs of the faithful in addition
to and alongside of the liturgy. As such, the better
understanding and use of the liturgy will not do
away with this type of prayer. It will emerge in
a renewed or revised form as needed by the faithful. Already the rise of Charismatic prayer gives
every indication of being such a work of the Spirit,
at least in some of its aspects.

Having said that, one is ready to seek out both
the strengths and weaknesses of liturgical and extra-
liturgical prayer, before going to seek principles
for the renewal of popular devotions and other
forms of non-liturgical prayer.

LITURGICAL AND DEVOTIONAL PRAYER

Liturgical prayer is strong because it is anchored in Scripture, in central truths, in the essentials (Mass and the

Sacraments) and in the Liturgical Year. It is communal, objective and durable. Devotional prayer is supportive of the liturgy, relates to some central truths, is warmly personal potentially (and often actually), is communal and is very adaptable. Both types of prayer are useful and strengthen each other.

PRINCIPLES FOR RENEWING PARALITURGICAL PRAYER

The *Constitution on the Sacred Liturgy* (n. 13) calls for the renewal of popular devotions, but it does not give the specific principles for that renewal. Fortunately, we can gather those principles from other official sources.

Two important documents for this purpose, are: (1) Pope Paul VI's Apostolic Exhortation, *Marian Devotions*, dated February 2, 1974; and (2) *Holy Communion and Worship of the Eucharist Outside Mass*, one of the last parts of the *Roman Ritual*, issued by the Congregation for Divine Worship, on June 21, 1973. To these fine documents, we should add a third by the great liturgist, Josef Jungmann— who always had a sincere respect for popular devotions: his chapter, *Guiding Principles for Devotions* in *The Good News Yesterday and Today*, W.H. Sadlier, (New York, 1962), pages 132-150.

When composing new prayers and paraliturgical services, we should be careful to involve all of these principles in the work, if possible. When dealing with older and beloved formulas of prayer, one can often use a prayer from the liturgical books in conjunction with these old prayers to update them.

Although it is theoretically possible to add appropriate lines to older prayers, to bring them into greater conformity to the norms of the liturgy, the pastoral effect of such additions on the people should be carefully gauged and, perhaps, an alternate solution selected. Novena and other well-defined prayer services should be considered as a whole, and the appropriate changes introduced somewhere in the over-all service.

With the three above-mentioned sources in mind, one could outline the following "principles".

1. *The Principle of Priority.*

Users and promoters of devotions and para-liturgies must distinguish between those elements which are essential and perennial, and those which are secondary and dated. One must continually go back to the unique origin and spirit of the devotion to learn the difference.

In practice, the writers and promoters of devotional prayer should go back regularly to the history of their own devotion, while at the same time being keen observers of the society in which they live. Only with both types of information in mind can they truly renew and continually update the devotion to meet the prayer needs of those who live in changing times and circumstances.

2. *The Trinitarian Principle.*

Christian prayer is worship offered to the Father,

to the Son, and to the Holy Spirit, One God in Three Persons. As the liturgy wisely illustrates, one prays to the Father through the mediation of the Son, with the assistance of the Holy Spirit. One of the providential signs of our times is a greater conscious awareness of the intervention of the Spirit in the life of the individual and of the Church.

In practice, one should model prayers on the well-known trinitarian approach of the liturgical prayers which are found in the Sacramentary, Liturgy of the Hours, and other official liturgical books of the Church. In both the hymns of the new and older Liturgy of the Hours (Breviary), one finds a wide variety of ways of doing this. This is particularly evident in the last stanza of the hymns. And not to be over-looked are the prayer formulas of the Eastern Rites, which face this same challenge and offer creative solutions for it.

3. *The Christological Principle.*

God the Father has created all persons and all things so that they may be handed over to Christ as their Head, Savior, Mediator, and Lord. Genuine Christian prayer never fails to relate all persons and things to the mediation and lordship of Christ: "through Christ our Lord". This essential relationship must always be kept in mind in all devotions to the Blessed Virgin and the Saints.

In practice, the appropriate and recommended way of praying is the liturgical manner: to the heavenly Father, through Christ our Lord, in union with the Holy Spirit. Many times this can be achieved by the insertion of few well-chosen phrases in otherwise well-written prayers. At other times it may be done by using a liturgical prayer in connection with devotional prayers (as the Liturgy of the Hours does by adding the priestly oration after an antiphon proper to the Virgin or Saint).

Some few times a total revision of the prayer may be required. But, one should be careful not to eliminate other legitimate, even if not the more common, approach to Almighty God: all sound prayer is of the Spirit. Even the liturgy itself offers some variations, especially when we consider all the rites of the Church.

4. *The Biblical Principle.*

Because the Bible is the word of God, it should be the well-spring and inspiration of all Christian prayers and devotions. It is the inspired example, model, and light of God for prayer and living.

In practice, one should use as much Scripture as possible in the composition of prayers, even using phrases from it in the preparation of the final text. (Naturally, one is not merely stringing bits of lines together, but rather being inspired by biblical prayer and using it as inspiration for creative prayer.) Scriptural readings, as the inspired word of God, would be used in preference to all other readings. Non-scriptural readings could be used in non-liturgical prayer, but they often serve better to state a theme, bring out a possible meaning of a passage, and application of it to the circumstances of everyday life. While the *Constitution on the Sacred Liturgy* (n. 35) encourages us to foster Bible Services, this should not be broadened to mean the reduction of all devotional services to

Bible ones. Each has its own unique value in the Church!

5. *The Liturgical Principle.*

All prayer and devotional activity should be inspired by the liturgy, lead to it, and flow from it. It should seek guidance and example from the liturgy, without being suppressed by or merged into the liturgy. The special character of the Eucharist should be maintained, and non-eucharistic devotions respected for their special services as auxiliaries to the liturgy.

In practice, the general norms of good liturgy should be studied and applied to all forms of prayer, without reducing those forms of prayer to liturgy. A special point should be made of relating a devotion to the liturgical season and to the Sunday liturgy. This is best done by using readings, prayers, and hymns from the Sunday or seasonal liturgy. It can be assisted by the use of popular hymns and religious customs (such as the Advent Wreath,) associated with the liturgical season.

Judicious use can be made of multi-media, sacred movement and dance, banners and hangings especially in non-liturgical activities, which are not as strictly bound by Church regulations. (A study should be made of local Church regulations on the use of media.)

Finally, while Benediction and Communion should be encouraged, this is not the same as saying that they should be taken as a matter of course whenever there is a paraliturgical service. This is especially true of services asking the intercession of the Blessed Virgin and the Saints. One should make obvious the eucharistic connection with such devotions. This can be done, for example, with the use of many of the Prayers over the Gifts and After Communion from for Masses of the Virgin and Saints. (The Liturgical Commission of Baltimore has prepared an excellent planning guide to the new Sacramentary entitled, *Through Christ our Lord.*)

6. *The Ecclesial Principle.*

Because God has established a Church through Christ as his chosen means of salvation, prayer must bear this relationship of man's salvation in community. The riches of the mystery of the Church should appear in prayer: e.g. the Church as institution, Mystical Body, People and Family of God.

In practice, one should guard against an overly individualistic and subjective approach to prayer. Somewhere in the content of the prayer one should find indications of the mystery of the Church. A good model of this is found in the ending of some Eastern Rite prayers: "through Christ our Lord in the midst of his Church...."

One should also use the Bidding Prayers or Prayers of the Faithful in the spirit of the liturgical books: for the needs of the Church, the Pope, bishops, civic leaders, universal and local needs, etc. (Priests and religious should be generous in sharing the use of their liturgical books—especially the Sacramentary and the Liturgy of the Hours—so that liturgical planning teams can learn at first hand what the Church considers good communal prayers.

43

Good hand missals are now available for such use too.)

7. *The Ecumenical Principle.*

A hallmark of modern times is the effort made among Christians to achieve some measure of unity in Christ. While not sacrificing the purity of the Catholic faith, great care should be exercised in the writing or selection of prayers to be used in all inter-faith services. Common elements and readings should be favored, which are rooted in solid doctrine and inspired by the Scriptures.

In practice, one's attitude and choice of words is rather important in all ecumenical encounters. With a heart filled with charity and truth, one would prepare for such services with foresight based on the religious sensitivity and outlook of those who will participate. In an inter-faith service, one would avoid or use with extreme prudence those ideas and practices on which Christians have traditionally differed. Even when used among ourselves, such things should be carefully explained so that a reasonable and accurate answer can be given when questions arise in mixed groups.

8. *The Anthropological Principle.*

Truth is one, and there is no real conflict between the concepts of prayer and science. While the supernatural goes beyond the ambit of the natural, it should be aware of its psycho-social outlook.

In practice, the way one speaks about man and the world in prayer should not become dated, but rather be kept abreast of the advances and insights of true science. If the prayer is to make any sense to the person of good will, then it must be aware of his or her thought-patterns, world-outlook, and manner of expressing them. Prayer words and concepts must be continually evaluated to see if they really convey to the person hearing them what the prayer intends to convey.

Even biblical pastoral images must be examined in this light, so that they make sense to the Christian living in an urban setting. Images of the contemporary world have largely been unused as suitable means of reaching the divine; for example: speed, movement, motors, production, computers, light, and so on. (While St. Francis de Sales wrote in the 17th Century, the enduring value of his insights are not tied to the unique language of his times and could be judiciously transferred to the language of any time and place.)

These general principles for renewing devotional prayer should be continually in mind when writing, promoting, and using popular devotions and group prayer. They can be employed as well on personal prayers.

When used on existing devotions, the tone and the service as a whole should be considered, rather than just the single prayer by themselves.

SOME PRACTICAL POINTS

First, it is always best to begin one's preparation for a paraliturgy by selecting a theme suitable for the occasion, group, and liturgical season. All the elements of the prayer service should fit into and advance this theme.

Second, outline the general format of the service from the start. In the guidelines offered in the document, *Holy Communion and Worship of the Eucharist Outside of Mass,* one finds the direction: "... there should be prayers, songs, and readings. A homily or brief exhortation should follow the readings from Scripture ... It is desirable for the people to respond by singing and to spend some time in religious silence" (n. 95). A *sample order of service* might be:

(1) Opening song or ceremonies;

(2) Statement of theme;

(3) Opening Prayer;

(4) Reading(s) and response(s);

(5) Period of silence;

(6) Homily or short explanation;

(7) Special and intercessory prayers;

(8) The Lord's Prayer and Sign of Peace or other "sign", "action" or ceremony;

(9) (Possible Benediction or Communion);

(10) Concluding prayer, song, or ceremony.

We should use a little imagination to introduce variety from time to time, i.e. sing with organ, guitar, or other instrument, or simply listen to the instrument(s), solo or in concert. The musical styling can be traditional, folk or contemporary. The praying and singing can be done together with the celebrant, alternating in groups, or alone. The prayers themselves can come from Western and Eastern prayer traditions—with suitable adaptation and introductions. Sacred gesture, dance, and multimedia can be used in accord with local liturgical readiness and regulation.

Third, first select the key prayer (s), reading (s), and action (s), and then build the rest of the prayer service around them.

Fourth, the degree of public participation should be planned.

Fifth, adequate provisions should be made for satisfying individual needs through periods of silent prayer, special prayers (i.e. novena prayers, and provisions for adding petitions to the Prayers of the Faithful).

Sixth, some unique "action" or sacramental should be included to arouse interest and reinforce the theme. This might be the use of a liturgical symbol, a religious custom, a procession, banner, or other ceremony. Its relationship with the theme is of paramount importance and should be easily comprehended.

Finally, participation aids should be prepared for the community: an attractively printed Order of

Service, with correct page number in the hymnals or other books to be used, and so on. The services of a lector, server, and musician should be lined up. The appearance of the leader of prayer and place of the prayer are important too.

PRAYERS BY SAINTS

A GENERAL PRAYER:

O Lord, keep us in Thy ways,
direct us in Thy paths,
recall our wanderings,
make us to hear Thy voice
with gladness and to rejoice
in Thy salvation. Amen.

(St. Elizabeth Seton, 1774-1821.)

PRAYER TO BE GOD'S INSTRUMENT OF PEACE:

Lord, make me an instrument of your peace!
Where there is hatred, let me sow love;
Where there is injury, pardon;
Where there is doubt, faith;
Where there is despair, hope;
Where there is darkness, light;
Where there is sadness, joy.
O divine Master,
grant me not so much to seek

to be consoled as to console,
to be understood as to understand,
to be loved as to love.
    For it is in giving that we receive;
it is in pardoning that we are pardoned;
and it is in dying
that we are born to eternal life. Amen.

    (St. Francis of Assisi, c. 1181-1226) *

FOR STRENGTH FROM CHRIST:

    Christ be with me,
Christ before me, Christ behind me,
Christ in me.
    Christ beneath me, Christ above me,
Christ on my right, Christ on my left,
Christ where I lie, Christ where I sit,
Christ where I rise.
    Christ in the heart of every man who thinks
                                        of me.
Christ in the mouth of every man who speaks
                                        of me.
Christ in every eye that sees me.
Christ in every ear that hears me.
    Salvation is of Christ.
May your salvation, Lord, be ever with us. Amen.

    (The Armor of St. Patrick, d. 492.)

---

* Those prayers commonly attributed to a Saint are accepted
  as such.

50

FAVORITE PRAYER OF A SAINT:

Great God of all glory, and you, my Lord Jesus Christ: I beg of you to illumine me and to dissipate the darkness of my spirit, to give me our faith, firm hope, and perfect charity. O my God, grant me to know you well and to do all things according to your will. Amen.

(St. Francis of Assisi, c. 1181-1226.)

MEDIEVAL PRAYER TO CHRIST:

Thank you, Lord Jesus Christ,
for all the benefits and blessings which you have
given me,
for all the pains and insults which you have
borne for me.
Merciful Friend, Brother, and Redeemer,
may I know you more clearly,
love you more dearly,
and follow you more nearly, day by day.

(St. Richard of Chichester, d. 1253.)

PRAYER FOR GENEROSITY:

Teach me, good Lord, to serve you as you
deserve:
to give and not count the cost;
to fight and not heed the wounds;
to toil and not seek for rest;
to labor and not seek for reward,
save that of knowing that I do your will. Amen.

(St. Ignatius Loyola, c. 1491-1556.)

PRAYER OF COMMITMENT:

Take, Lord, all my liberty, my memory, my understanding, and all my will. You have bestowed on me whatever I have; I give it all back to you and deliver it to you, to be entirely subject to your will. Give me only your love and your grace, and I am rich enough, and ask for nothing more. Amen.

(St. Ignatius Loyola, c. 1491-1556.)

A MONK'S PRAYER:

O Gracious and Holy Father,
give us wisdom to perceive you;
intelligence to seek you;
eyes to behold you;
a heart to meditate upon you;
and a life to proclaim you,
through the power of the Spirit
of Jesus Christ our Lord. Amen.

(St. Benedict, c. 480 - c. 547.)

ON READING THE WORD OF GOD:

Shine in our hearts, Master who loves mankind, the pure light of your divine knowledge and open the eyes of our mind that we may understand the announcing of your Good News; set in us a reverence of your blessed commandments, so that trampling all carnal desires, we may begin to live according to the spirit, both willingly and doing everything for your pleasure.

For You are the light of our souls and bodies, Christ God, and we send up glory to You and to your eternal Father and to your all-holy, good and life-giving Spirit, now and always and for ever and ever. Amen.

(St. Basil the Great, 329-379.)

CONSECRATION AND PETITIONS:

Into your hands, O Lord, and into the hands of your Angels, I commit and entrust this day my soul, my relatives, my benefactors, my friends and my enemies and all the members of the Church. Preserve us, O Lord, this day, by the merits of the Blessed Virgin Mary and all the saints, from bad habits and evil inclinations, from sin and from the deceits of the devil, from a sudden and unprovided death, and from the pains of hell. Enlighten my heart by the grace of the Holy Spirit; grant that I may always keep your commandments, and permit not that I should be separated from you, who live and reign God, with the Father and the same Holy Spirit, for ever and ever. Amen.

(St. Edmond, d. 1240.)

PRAYER SUITABLE FOR EVENING:

Watch with those, O Lord,
who wake, or watch, or weep tonight,
and give your angels charge over those who sleep.
Tend your sick ones, O Lord Christ.
Rest your weary ones,
Bless your dying ones.

Soothe your suffering ones.
Pity your afflicted ones.
Shield your joyous ones,
and all for your love's sake. Amen.

(St. Augustine, 354-430.)

The secret of Catholicism's capacity to harmonize liturgical worship with the demands of personal devotion lies in the fact that both the one and the other are responses to the same reality.

(Dom Aelred Graham, 20th Century)

3

SACRED
HEART
DEVOTIONS

Have you ever heard of executing a statue? Well, the Communists did just that during the Spanish Civil War during the 1930's. In 1919 King Alfonso XIII and the Spanish bishops had consecrated their country to Christ and his Heart, and set up a large statue of the Sacred Heart in the suburb of "Cerro de los Angeles", just outside of Madrid.

When the Communists seized Madrid, they invited the world press to the execution of this statue of Christ and his Heart. The very thought of such an execution reveals how well they understood what Catholics claim is the essential characteristic of Christ's character—a loving Person. As such, He was and is the very antithesis of what they espoused.

For the recent popes, at least, devotion to Christ and his Heart is not just another devotion. It is most central! Pope Leo XIII called it "a most excellent form of religion"; Pope Pius XII called it "a most perfect way of professing the Christian religion"; and Pope Paul VI called it "an excellent and acceptable form of true piety ... especially because of the norms laid down in the Second Vatican Council". Modern theologians are seeing the devotion as a relationship to the redeeming love of Christ, and that love is at the very heart of the Christian religion.

WHAT IS DEVOTION TO THE HEART OF JESUS ?

Devotion to the Heart of Jesus is essentially a worshipful relationship to the Person of Christ, who is seen precisely from that ultimate understanding of him—which is that he is a loving Person. While both the love and the Heart of Christ can be called objects of this devotion, they must always be seen as representing and standing for the entire Person of Christ.

The physical Heart of the Risen Savior is singled out—at his request, but also long before, as a result of human reasoning—as the unique symbol of this mysterious love. It stands as a reminder to know and love Christ so well that one lives ever after, as it were, seeing life as he does—from the inside of his Heart outward. There can never be a question of relating to a part of Christ—even his Heart— apart from him. Devotion of this kind is always an adoration of and response to the loving Person who is Christ, under the aspect of, from the view point of, through the symbol of his Heart; that is, to Christ and his Heart.

SCRIPTURAL BASIS OF THE DEVOTION

Some people mistakenly think that devotion to the Sacred Heart only began with St. Margaret Mary Alacoque in the 17th Century. This is far from the truth. The devotion traces its origins back to the earliest days of the Church, to devotion to the wounds and the pierced side of Christ (John 19: 34).

Throughout the pages of Scripture, we find all the key ideas which are involved in devotion to the Heart of Jesus: the love of God for mankind, even to the sending of his beloved Son as Savior, the biblical use of the word "Heart" to stand for the deepest and most central to the person, and Christ's redemptive love for humankind. It is by placing all of these ideas together, within the limits of sound biblical exegesis, that one arrives at the biblical basis of this devotion.

Isaiah presents the love of God as so great that it is more than the impossible—that a mother would forget the infant that she bore (49: 14-15). Hosea likens God's love to a father's love and tenderness to his children, or to a husband's love even for an unfaithful wife (2: 9-27). Jeremiah saw God's love so strong that he would eventually write his covenant right in their very hearts and remember their sins no more (31: 31-34).

The Psalms often speak of God's love with the expressions of "mercy" and "kindness" and "loving-kindness" (18: 19; 69: 16; 103, 8: 117, 1-2; 146, 8). This same love of God is very clear from the parables of Jesus about the Good Shepherd (John 10: 1-21), the Lost Sheep (Luke 15:1-7), and the

Prodigal Father and Son (Luke 15: 11-32). The discourse at the Last Supper again brings out God's love, but especially in sending the beloved Son (John 15: 9-13). St. Paul takes up this theme of God's love, especially as expressed in Christ in his letters to the Romans (5: 7-8), to the Ephesians (1: 7-10; 3: 17-19) and elsewhere.

Such a message of love is clear to the believer. In the course of time, the devout meditation on the passages of Scripture linked part with part, to form a Scriptural basis for a theology and devotion to the Heart of Christ.

In this process, three Scripture quotations had particular importance. St. John records three incidents which the other evangelists do not record. First, one has the speech of Christ at the Feast of Tabernacles, when he shouted out: "If anyone thirsts, let him come to me: let him drink, who believes in me. Scripture has it: From within him rivers of living waters shall flow" (7: 35-41).

The second incident records the flow of blood and water, following the piercing of Christ's side by the Roman soldier (19: 34). And the third is the fact that the marks of the wounds in Jesus' side and hands are still a part of the Risen Lord (21: 25).

In seeking to unify all that one knows and believes about Christ, Christians have made that short step from thinking about the origin of all that Christ was and is, as well as all the blessings and graces which flow from him (the "living waters") to considering the Heart within the wounded side as the symbol of this unique Person and all God's great love for us in Christ.

While such thinking in the past was not sufficiently presented to the ordinary person, yet it existed. When Pope Pius XII issued his call to scholars—in his masterful encyclical on the Heart of Jesus (*Haurietis Aquas*, 1956)—this was carefully done. These men of learning presented the scriptural, patristic, liturgical, and historical bases for the devotion, and it harmonizes well with developments in Scripture and theology. The loving Savior, having undergone his Paschal death and glorification, is the same Risen Lord, who is the object of this devotion.

HISTORY OF THE DEVOTION

There are many commentaries of early Christian writers, the Fathers of the Church, on the three important texts from John's Gospel mentioned above. They saw in the pierced side—as the Second Vatican Council did later in its *Dogmatic Constitution on the Church,* n. 3—the sign and origin of the Church, the sacraments, and all the graces which flow to us from Christ.

Between 800-1000, this devotion developed from warm devotion to the humanity and wounds of Christ into a more definite form of using the Heart of the Redeemer as a symbol of God's love for us revealed in Christ. Among Eastern Rite Catholics, the beautiful word, "philanthropia" (love of mankind), was used in reference to devotion to God's love.

While Eastern art adapted a well-known icon,

with Christ blessing with one hand and holding the Gospel book in the other, by adding the expressive words "All of you who are burdened come to me" on the book, Western art began to openly show the Heart. The Medieval mystic saw in the Heart a unique resting place and source of love. Medieval theologians began to write of this devotion and the laity practiced it first under the form of devotion to the Five Wounds.

During the 16th Century, many people saw in the devotion a heart-warming answer to the division, confusion, and heart-aches which were a part of the Reformation. Some years before Christ appeared to St. Margaret Mary Alacoque between 1673-1675, St. John Eudes worked to promote the liturgical celebrations in honor of the Hearts of Jesus and Mary.

In 1673, Christ appeared to St. Margaret Mary to complain of the indifference, coldness, and contempt which so many people exhibited towards him in return for all the love which he had for them. He asked her to promote devotion specifically to his Heart as the symbol of the love of his Person for all men and women. He also requested Communions received in a spirit of reparation—particularly on the *First Fridays* of the month, for holy hours, and other forms of devotion.

In extending these loving invitations, Christ promised many blessings, especially the grace not to die out of his favor if one received Communion on the nine First Fridays. (Some modern Christians are bothered by these promises—probably by the bad example of people who "made the Nine First Fridays" and then thought that they had some

sort of hold over God to act as they pleased thereafter. Everyone should know that Christ never
meant that! The Lord only shows us how anxious
he is for our love by all that he promised to get
it. But, he promised as much for absolute faith in
the Gospel (Matthew 17: 20), as well as for the
loving reception of the Eucharist (John 6: 54).
Now he also attaches it to devotion to his Heart.)

THE ENDURING VALUE
OF THE DEVOTION

While Karl Rahner—the great German theologian
before, during, and after the Council—judges that
this devotion was given for the ills of modern
times (that is, the gradual secularization of so
many facets of society, the elimination of Christian
religious values from modern life, the rise of athe-
ism and agnosticism with its inward and outward
"absence of God"), it has the *enduring value* of
understanding the redemptive love of Christ and
responding with love in turn.

This is all the more cogent, since the person who
responds to Christ in love knows that he or she
is most sincerely loved in return—and in the first
place. "God became our brother so that everyone
would feel that he was in God's thoughts and in
God's Heart" (Pope Paul VI).

RELATIONSHIP WITH THE LITURGY

All forms of devotion to the Risen Lord, who comes among his people in that special way which is the Eucharistic celebration, only reach their flowering—or should reach it—in the Mass. The same is no less true of this devotion. The same Heart which beat during the earthly part of Christ's life and which he has in heavenly glory is sacramentally present in the Eucharist. (Care must be taken, though, not to think of his unique presence there as ordinary human presence. It is whole and entire, body and soul, humanity and divinity, but now in a sacramental manner.

Devotion to the Eucharistic Heart of Christ practices devotion to the Heart of the Lamb from the special aspect of the Eucharist, as well as sees the Eucharist as one of the special acts of Christ's love for his Church. In addition to this consideration, the Church itself has placed this devotion in the liturgy with a special Solemnity of the Sacred Heart and the possibility of Votive Masses to Christ and his Heart on First Fridays and the frequent open weekdays of the year.

As will be seen below, all the devotional practices of this response to Christ have also been sacramentalized, but the words of the Preface best call us to respond to Christ's love: "Lift up your hearts".

SUGGESTIONS FOR UPDATING THE DEVOTION

Providentially, with the encyclical of Pope Pius XII on the Sacred Heart in 1956, this devotion has been given an early start in updating its practices. The only real problem is to transfer this vast body of material from the books and journals where it appeared into the heads and hearts of the faithful. These general suggestions could be made for renewal of the devotion.

First, while respecting the great work done by St. Margaret Mary Alacoque in popularizing a particular form of the devotion (and image of Christ), one should distinguish the essential elements from particular forms given to the devotion. (There have been many down through the centuries!)

After understanding that this devotion is to the love of God revealed and existing in the Person of Christ, one can be open to a wholesome pluralism of ways to respond to this love. While the physical Heart is still the symbol of his great love for us, there are many useful historic forms, as well as creative, newer forms of response to Christ's loving invitation for our love and service.

Second, all traditional practices of the devotion should be used in their newer, sacramentalized forms. To be sacramentalized means to have some definite relationship to the Eucharist and the other sacraments. For example, the *Daily Offering* has always been a giving of our "prayers, works, joys and sufferings" to Christ in the Mass. In the deeper awareness of what the eucharistic celebration means in the life of Christ and his Church, one should more deliberately anchor his or her life in the Mass—as liturgical piety strongly urges.

Reparation to Christ and his Heart must include efforts to make up for unfaithful love beyond formulas of "Acts of Reparation" to include all that is implied in reconciliation. There must be a turning to God, a change of heart, and—within and apart from the "Sacrament of Reconciliation"— every effort to be at one and restored to communion with God, our neighbors (the community), and ourselves.

The *First Friday* will be seen as both an additional opportunity that week to take part in the sacramental representation of the paschal mystery of Christ's death and resurrection, as well as one to express love for all men, most especially the sinner, in this sacramental way. The day Friday itself should continue to be our special day of loving praise and gratitude for all the blessings and graces which flowed from the Heart of the Lamb on Good Friday.

Holy Hours can be thought of as occasions when we can satisfy our deep hunger for Christ's friendship and love. While these hours of prayer can have periods of prayers of reparation, they should especially offer us time to listen as well as speak to God.

Prayers of *Consecration* are now rooted more consciously in the sacraments of Baptism, Confirmation, and Wedding or Ordination commitments. While it all begins with Baptism, regular renewal of the baptismal vows or other commitments urged us to be more constant and willing to make these sacraments more effective in our lives. All in all, then, each devotional practice has some link with the sacraments and helps us to put on Christ more consciously through liturgical and devotional piety.

Finally, one should be open to the possibility of other images of Christ and his Heart. The traditional image of Christ in white robe and red mantle, with his Heart on his chest, is not of the essence of this devotion. While one should respect those who find it meaningful, nevertheless, everyone should respect a wholesome pluralism of tastes and needs in regard to pictures, statues and other images of Christ.

As long as the Heart is indicated in some way, there are more possibilities for such images than we now have. Some people are finding the Eastern Rite icon of "Jesus Christ, Lover of Mankind" effective for them. Some respond to more contemporary presentations of Christ with a simpler, stylized Heart.

Others are seeing in the original presentation of Christ with pierced side the symbol of his love. As long as there is some indication of the Heart or mark of the wounded side, one has the visible symbol of the "heart-center" (Karl Rahner) of all that was and is Christ, the Lover of Mankind.

SACRED HEART PRAYERS

PRAYERS FROM THE LITURGY

Father,
we rejoice in the gifts of love
we have received from the heart of
   Jesus your Son.
Open our hearts to share his life
and continue to bless us with
   his love.
We ask this through our Lord
   Jesus Christ, your Son,
who lives and reigns with you
   and the Holy Spirit,
one God, for ever and ever. Amen.

(Sacramentary, Solemnity of the Sacred Heart)

ALTERNATE PRAYER: REPARATION THEME

Father,
we have wounded the heart of Jesus your Son,
but he brings us forgiveness and grace.

Help us to prove our grateful love
and make amends for our sins.
We ask this...... (above).

(Sacramentary, Solemnity of the Sacred Heart)

CONTEMPORARY PRAYER OF CONSECRATION

Father of our Lord Jesus Christ, we thank you for creating us, still more for restoring us to your grace, and for giving us the gifts of love which we have received from you through the Heart of your Son. We thank you for the gifts of your Spirit, the Church, the Sacraments, and all your graces. We praise you for all your love and goodness to us.

We wish to prove our grateful love by offering you our hearts. Remove from us whatever hinders us from becoming truly one with you; increase our strength of will for doing good; open our minds to receive your Spirit; and turn our hearts to follow Christ's path of love-filled service to others. We ask this in faith and in Christ's name. Amen.

TRADITIONAL ACT OF CONSECRATION

O most holy Heart of Jesus, fountain of every blessing, I adore you, I love you, and with a lively sorrow for my sins, I offer you this poor heart of mine. Make me humble, patient, pure, and wholly obedient to your will. Grant, good Jesus, that I may live in you and for you. Protect me in the midst of danger; comfort me in my afflictions; give me health of body; assistance in my temporal needs; your blessings on all that I do; and the grace of a holy death. (Amen.)

69

*You live and reign with the Father and the Holy Spirit, one God, for ever and ever. Amen.

(Raccolta, 263.)

CONSECRATION OF A FAMILY

Lord Jesus Christ, we consecrate to you today ourselves and our family. The love for us and for all men that fills your Heart prompts us to pledge our lives in return.

We wish to live our lives in union with you. We wish to share your mission of bringing your Father's love to all men. We wish you to be the center of our hearts and of our home.

Lord Jesus Christ, accept this consecration of our family to you, and keep us ever one in your most Sacred Heart. Amen.

(Irish Apostleship of Prayer)

CONTEMPORARY PRAYER OF REPARATION

Lord Jesus Christ, we look at the Cross, and we, your pilgrim Church, can see what sin has done to the Son of Mary, to the Son of God. But now you are risen and glorified. You suffer no more in the flesh. Sin can no longer expose you to the agony in the garden, to the scourging, to death on a cross.

---

* This is the special ending for liturgical prayers which are addressed to the Son. It is fitting to add them to all devotional prayers addressed to Jesus Christ.

70

But it can reach you through your Mystical Body. This part of you, your Church on earth, still feels the strength of sin. For this we make our act of reparation.

We, who have sinned in the past, now consecrate ourselves to the healing of your Mystical Body, to our part in the mystery of its well-being and its growth. Sanctify us for this task.

May your Sacred Heart be the symbol, not of one love but two—your love for us and ours for you. Accept our love, and help us make it real by serving you in our brothers, so that love and concern may lead all men "to know the one true God and Jesus Christ whom he has sent". Amen.

(Apostleship of Prayer)

TRADITIONAL ACT OF REPARATION

My loving Jesus, out of grateful love I bear you, and to make reparation for my unfaithfulness to grace, I give you my heart, and I consecrate myself wholly to you; and with the help of your grace I propose to sin no more. Amen. (1807.)

EASTERN RITE PRAYER

O Lord our God, whose power is without compare, whose glory is incomprehensible, whose mercy is beyond measure and whose love for mankind is beyond word: be pleased, Master, in the depths of your compassion, to look down on us and on this holy place, and make us and those praying with

71

us obtain the riches of your mercies and your tender pity.

For all glory, honor, and worship are your due, Father, Son, and Holy Spirit now and always and for ever and ever. Amen.

(Liturgy of St. Basil the Great)

SHORT PRAYERS: ASPIRATIONS

All for you, most Sacred Heart of Jesus.

*Jesus, meek and humble of Heart;
    make my heart like your Heart.*

Heart of Jesus, I put my trust in you.

May the Heart of Jesus be loved everywhere.

(Raccolta, 234, 227, 226, 223.)

READINGS FOR PARALITURGIES

Deut 7: 6-11	Romans 5: 5-11
Ezechiel 34: 11-16	Ephesians 1: 3-10
Hosea 11: 1-9	Ephesians 3: 8-12
Isaiah 49	Ephesians 3: 14-19
Psalm 23	Philippians 1: 8-11
Psalm 25	I John 4: 7-16
Psalm 34	Matthew 11: 25-30
	Luke 15: 1-10, 11-32
	John 7: 34-41
	John 10: 11-18
	John 15: 1-8; 9-17
	John 19: 31-34

4

THE EUCHARIST OUTSIDE OF MASS

If one takes a nice morning drive north out of Rome, Italy, he arrives at the city of Orvieto—built on a little plateau. Some Americans know the name from the fine white wine made from the grapes grown around the city. Many Italians know the city because of its beautiful Corpus Christi Procession.

In 1264, Pope Urban VI was in residence in the city, and he proclaimed this feast, "The Feast of the Eucharist" (Festum Eucharistiae), a festival day for the universal Church. In remembrance of this famous event in its history, the townspeople conduct one of the finest liturgical celebrations anywhere in the country.

After celebrating Mass in the cathedral, a long and colorful procession escorts the Blessed Sacrament around the streets of Orvieto for Benediction at three outdoor altars. Pages with trumpets warn the people who could not get inside the cathedral for the start of the procession. Knights and soldiers dressed in the clothing of the 1200's come first;

then follow men with banners to represent the guilds and organizations of medieval Orvieto. The town officials come next in period costume.

The school children from public and private schools follow next in line in their characteristic smocks. The First Holy Communion and Confirmation classes of the year appear. Then sodalities and married people's groups. The orphans appear. These are followed by the religious orders and congregations which serve in the city. The clergy come last with the bishop carrying the Blessed Sacrament. It is a magnificent sign of the people's great love for Christ in the Blessed Sacrament.

It is such a strange contrast to the other event of that same century on the Eucharist. In the early part of that century, the Fourth Lateran Council made it obligatory that all members of the Church had to go to Confession and Holy Communion once a year during the Easter time (Canon 21). One can only imagine how infrequently people were going previous to this time!

And even though the people desired to honor Christ in the Sacred Host outside of Mass, it took a long time for this decree of the Fourth Lateran Council to be fully observed. How strange! Desiring to honor Christ in the Eucharist, but not wishing to bring Christ-in-the-Eucharist within their hearts!

HISTORY OF EUCHARISTIC DEVOTION

Many people remember the days just prior to the Second Vatican Council, when people dropped into church for a visit to the Blessed Sacrament or participated in the frequent evening devotional services which normally ended with Benediction. At that time, it was not the practice of the Church to allow evening Masses.

When this regulation was changed, most churches —without any great consultation of the people— only scheduled evening Masses thereafter. Liturgists, like Josef Jungmann, now suggest that perhaps our eucharistic piety, and even our participation in the Mass itself, would profit much by some preparatory activity—like eucharistic devotion outside of Mass.

The eucharistic devotions which so many remember—visits to the Blessed Sacrament, Benediction, Forty Hours, Corpus Christi Processions, Nocturnal Adoration, Eucharistic Congresses, and so forth— are products of the last eight or nine hundred years of church history.

In the early Church, there was a slightly different emphasis on the Eucharist, and, so, a different way in which it was expressed. While believing in the fact that the Eucharist was really Christ's Body and Blood, they centered their piety and practical living on a deep conscious awareness of the Body of Christ which is the Church: Jesus was really present in the Eucharist, but he continued to exist in his Body mystically.

There are few documents to attest to how the faithful related to the eucharistic bread which they were permitted to bring home to the sick, and to communicate themselves throughout the week. With the Eucharist present in their homes all week, there had to be some relationship with the sacramental presence of Christ. Because we have no records from the ordinary faithful of this period, we do not know what it was. It would be wrong to read into the situation our attitude towards "visiting" the Blessed Sacrament, but one wonders if there was a warm relationship, or at least passing prayers like aspirations, to recognize that presence.

Justin the Martyr mentions that the Eucharist was reserved for the sick around the year 150 A.D. From the 4th Century onward, the Eucharist was kept in the church or sacristy. The custom of taking it home was discontinued rather early because of abuses, but the little wooden, metal, or ivory boxes used for doing so became the beginnings of our pyx and ciborium—vessels for holding sacred bread.

Only in the 9th Century do we find definite regulations about them. The shape of these receptacles for the Eucharist changed from box-shape to polygon to circular. With the 13th Century, one finds stem and base added—like a chalice. The container for the Eucharist was not always locked up in a cupboard or safe. In France and England, during the late Middle Ages, one finds the pyx suspended from the ceiling of the church.

Sometimes it had the appearance of a steeple-like turret or even of a dove. The pyx was sometimes placed under a trumpet-like canopy and was called a "hanging pyx". When the dove-shaped container was used, one opened the back of the bird to take out the Eucharist. When unleavened bread replaced the more ancient practice of leavened species, larger containers were produced by metal-smiths—like the present type of ciborium: melon-shaped receptacle, with cover, stem, and base.

The pyx or ciborium was eventually kept in a

safe cabinet. Sometimes this appeared in the shape of a cupboard partly sunk into the wall, as a somewhat free-standing sacrament-house, and, eventually, as a locked cabinet on the side altar. By the 16th Century, the tabernacle was placed on the main altar—where it became the familiar part of the pre-conciliar sanctuary.

The devotion of the ordinary person to the Eucharist changed as the forms of understanding of the Eucharist changed. In the early Church, people went to Communion as often as they went to the Eucharistic celebration. To be deprived of the privilege of receiving the Eucharist meant to be "excommunicated". They received Communion weekly at the liturgy, received the sacred species in their hands, and took some of It home with them for reception during the week.

When they prayed, "give us this day our bread", they literally meant their spiritual bread as well as their ordinary food—taking one immediately after the other. Gradually, though, people received the Eucharist less and less. By the 8th-9th Centuries, people rarely went to the Table of the Lord. White and unleavened bread replaced the more ancient forms, and the posture for receiving standardized into kneeling. An attitude of unworthiness, among other reasons, pervaded the soul of the ordinary person.

More and more was written about the real presence of Christ in the Eucharist, though, and this caused a change in devotional practices. By the 12th Century, there was a great desire to see the Host at the Consecration in the Mass. By the 13th Century, the elevation at that time became important to the people. As heretics attacked some aspect of the Church's teaching on the Eucharist, the people reacted to it in their piety at Mass.

When the doctrine of Transubstantiation was attacked by some of the reformers, the elevation assumed an even greater value to the people. They even spoke of it as "visible Communion" and, sometimes, went from one altar to another to be present at the elevation of the Host. (Records even indicate that some—how many?—just came to Church for this part of the Mass only and left immediately afterwards!) With the Council of Trent, one finds a real attempt to urge people to receive Communion very regularly, and not be satisfied with "visible communion".

The introduction of the Feast of Corpus Christi in 1264 partly fits into this general atmosphere. Since the remembrance of the institution of the Eucharist on Holy Thursday was effected by the sorrowful memories of the Agony in the Garden and Good Friday that same week, there was also a desire to honor the Eucharist in a more joyful way outside of the Lenten season. Hence, we have a blend of several needs giving rise to a new expression of Eucharistic piety.

In contrast to the "dynamic action" of Christ offering himself and his followers to his Father in the Sacrifice of the Mass, the liturgist could call adoration of Christ present in the Eucharist a "static" action, but it had its own inspiration from the Holy Spirit. Rather than reduce the Church's eucharistic practice to the Mass and nothing more, one should be open to all that is of the Spirit. While deficient elements in this pluralism of eucharistic practices should be improved, nevertheless, it is a bounty which should be offered so that the needs of all can be satisfied.

RELATIONSHIP TO THE LITURGY

Devotion to the Eucharist outside of Mass has a very definite relationship to the liturgy. The Church has enunciated her teaching on the Mass and Eucharistic piety in a whole series of official documents. The important ones are: *On the Eucharist* (Mystery of Faith) (1965); *The Instruction on Eucharistic Worship* (1967); *The General Instructions* for the Sacramentary (1969); and *Holy Communion and Worship of the Eucharist Outside of Mass* (1973). The second and fourth documents mentioned parallel each other in their treatment of devotions concerning the Eucharist. A few lines will summarize that teaching very clearly.

"The eucharistic sacrifice," we read in the 1973 document, "is the source and culmination of the whole Christian life. Both private and public devotion toward the eucharist, therefore, including devotion outside of Mass, are strongly encouraged when celebrated according to the regulations of lawful authority."

"In the arrangement of devotional services of this kind," continues Section 79, "the liturgical seasons should be taken into account. Devotions should be in harmony with the sacred liturgy in some sense, take their origin from the liturgy, and lead the people back to the liturgy".

The most important principle to remember in eucharistic piety is then given in Section 80:

"When the faithful honor Christ present in this sacrament, they should remember that this presence is derived from the sacrifice and is directed toward sacramental communion." If one understands this properly, he or she will unite in his or her practical living a full participation in the Mass—with Communion as a completion of the sacrifice, means to union with Christ and one another, and source of spiritual life and strength—as well as loving relationship with Christ present sacramentally after Mass.

One lives with the Lord in close familiarity, speaks to him of his or her cares and joys, petitions for the needs of the Church and one's dear ones, and in faith, hope, and love is drawn to receive Christ in the eucharistic celebration.

"Prayers before Christ the Lord sacramentally present", continues the above-quoted document, "extends the union with Christ which the faithful have reached in communion. It renews the covenant which in turn moves them to maintain in their lives what they have received by faith and by sacraments. They should try to lead their whole lives with the strength derived from the heavenly food, as they share in the death and resurrection of the Lord. Everyone should be concerned with good deeds and with pleasing God so that he or she may imbue the world with the Christian spirit and be a witness of Christ in the midst of human society" (n. 81).

The *enduring value* of devotion to the Eucharist outside of Mass, is to acknowledge Christ's continuing presence in this sacrament, be a means to greater spiritual union with the Lord and his entire body of members, prolong the effects of the Mass throughout the day and week, and provide pastorally for those who have been unable to participate in the eucharistic celebration with the rest of the community.

UPDATING EUCHARISTIC DEVOTIONAL PRACTICES

Visits to the Blessed Sacrament.

Since Christ is truly present sacramentally in the Holy Eucharist after Mass, it is only natural to offer him our honor and adoration. This honor has taken on many forms, according to the time and place where it was offered. Eastern Rite Catholics and oriental people find their ordinary gesture of respect—the deep bow—very proper in their relationship to Christ present in the Eucharist. The Catholics of Europe, and all the areas eventually settled by them, have a preference for the genuflection. (They may even tip their hats or bow their heads as they pass a church.)

While Christ is the perfect friend, who is infinitely purer and more helpful than our other friends, one should be careful not to visualize or treat that presence as the ordinary kind of human presence. It is of the sacramental order! It is a nearness, but also a "distance"—the very otherness of the Second Person of the Blessed Trinity, who is still God even though he has established this unique immanence. While acknowledging Christ as Friend, one must also relate to him as Eternal High Priest, sacrificial gift, continual nourishment, and liberator from human limitations.

This unique presence must also be related to the other presences of God in our lives, which the *Constitution on the Sacred Liturgy* (n. 7) and theology have pointed out for us. God is present as he keeps creation functioning in its various orders, as well as in the person in his love and grace—the "temples of the Holy Spirit" (I Cor. 3:16-17). Christ Lord is present "in the least of the brothers" (Matthew 25:40) and "where two or three gather in my name" (Matthew 18:20).

But, he is also present—as the Constitution (n. 7) tells us: in the Church, in her liturgical celebrations, in the sacrifice of the Mass—in the person of the priest, in his word, in the sacred species; in the sacraments; in the Scriptures read in Church; whenever the Church prays and sings. While it is hard to keep all of these presences in mind or to imagine them, they are all very real. Christ is "especially present" in the Eucharist (n. 7), but one should learn to appreciate the other modes of his presence away from the Place of Reservation.

Adoration of Christ in the Eucharist does present some ecumenical challenges in our relationships with those who do not share these same insights. Rather than discontinue these devotional practices, one should better explain them. Any person of good will always respects the sincere religious practices of others, even though he may not share them.

In an updated form, with adequate recognition of the forms of God's presence which others relate to, our eucharistic devotions can be respected by others. They will also remind Christians of the tensions of division and urge them to continue to work for greater unity.

Perhaps talk of visits to the Blessed Sacrament seems outdated in the light of so many locked churches. While not admitting that a locked church is the most creative answer to the problem—since a glass inclosure within the vestibule of most churches could be constructed—the locked doors can also stand as a symbol of the times we have excluded Christ through deliberate sin, as well as the exclusion which is part of the "coldness, neglect, and indifference" Christ complained about at Paray-le-Monial, France.

He specifically asked St. Margaret Mary Alacoque to promote reception of the Eucharist in a spirit of reparation on the First Fridays of the month to make up for being locked out of so many hearts. This is a definite request from his Heart.

Exposition and Benediction.

Exposition of the Blessed Sacrament is historically related to the people's desire to see the Host at Mass. Exposition is merely a longer period of adoration. If it is followed by a blessing with the Host, it is called Benediction.

From the 14th Century onward, one finds "exposition" occasionally at Mass. In the 15th Century, Benediction took place and was recorded at Hildesheim, Germany. Benediction was part of the Forty Hours Devotions—spread over three days to counteract the excesses of the carnivals just prior to

Lent—and of the Corpus Christi celebrations which often included Benediction at three outdoor altars. In more recent times, few afternoon or evening devotional services ended without Benediction.

The practice, though, was as open to deficient use as any other service conducted by and for human beings! Sometimes Benediction was given immediately after Mass, for the sole purpose of giving the blessing. So, the whole concept of the enduring presence of Christ after Mass was treated insufficiently in the process. Sometimes it took place within the Mass, without due regard for the sacrificial element of the Mass in progress. Sometimes it literally was in competition with the Mass, since it was often surrounded with more solemnity and popular participation than the Mass itself. (Some people substituted such devotions and Benediction for the Mass itself!) Hence, the Church itself was rather hesitant to give Benediction too free a reign.

In fact, one needed the permission of the bishop to conduct Benediction on most occasions until rather recently. And only in 1958 did the first Roman document declare that Benediction was a true liturgical action (Instruction on Sacred Music). Since the Eastern Rites of the Catholic Church center their eucharistic piety on the original dynamic element of the Sacred Liturgy, they understood, but did not follow too widely the Western tradition.

The use of music and singing, the blend of the symbol of incense with a large degree of participation, and the adoration and blessing of Christ sacramentally present still offers this service the possibility of being very meaningful and useful.

One may not use the fond hymns of the past ("Panis Angelicus", "O Salutaris Hostia", "Adore Te", or the "Tantum Ergo"), but the worship service can influence a newer generation as much as it did the older generation—at least on occasion.

The document, *Holy Communion and worship of the Eucharist Outside Mass* outlines for us the minimum updating expected by the Church.

Benediction may not take place at Mass. It may not be conducted for the sole purpose of giving the blessing with the host. Whenever it is scheduled immediately after Mass, the Host to be used should be consecrated at that Mass. It is to be set within a Liturgy of the Word with readings, songs, and periods of religious silence.

Exposition may take place for longer periods, and is recommended annually in churches where the Blessed Sacrament is regularly reserved. When this is done, it is directed that the sacrament be replaced in the tabernacle during periods when few people would be in church. It may be exposed again later at a scheduled time, when more people would be present.

Some of the new directives are rather specific ones.

For example, all genuflections before the Eucharist (exposed or not) are to be on *one* knee. We may have Benediction with either the ciborium or the monstrance. Incense, and from four to six candles are to be used with a monstrance; incense is optional and two candles are needed when the ciborium is used. Here is the basic outline of the renewed service of exposition and benediction:

1. The minister enters the sanctuary while a suitable hymn is sung.

2. He genuflects as he opens the tabernacle door and exposes the Blessed Sacrament.

3. He incenses the Eucharist if the Monstrance is used.

4. Prayer, reading, song, a possible homily or explanation, and sacred silence are used one or more times.

5. The minister returns to the altar and genuflects to the Blessed Sacrament.

6. Incense is used again, if the Monstrance is employed for Benediction. Meanwhile a eucharistic hymn is sung.

7. The minister sings or prays one of the liturgical prayers.

8. With humeral veil over his shoulders, he genuflects, takes up the Blessed Sacrament, and makes the sign of the cross with It over the people.

9. As he replaces the Eucharist in the tabernacle and genuflects, the people sing or recite an acclamation. (The once familiar "Divine Praises" are just one of *many* such acclamations which may be used. They are no longer prescribed at this time.)

10. During the final hymn or acclamation, the minister departs.

The word *minister* used above means the priest or deacon. The latter is empowered by the new regulations to celebrate Benediction.

The local bishop can also authorize a commissioned acolyte, a lay minister of the Eucharist, or even a member of a religious community or of a lay association which is devoted to eucharistic devotion to expose the Host. (They do not give the blessing with the Host, but replace It in the tabernacle—if they have received the necessary authorization.)

Since so many novena and devotional services traditionally end with Benediction, those who plan these devotions should take great care to relate the specific devotion to the eucharistic service to follow. Some connection should be carefully planned.

For this purpose, many of the Prayers over the Gifts and Prayers after Communion can easily be adapted. So often in the past, devotions to Mary and the Saints were followed by Benediction—without any specific preparation for or relationship with the Eucharist as Eucharist. Now this should be handled correctly.

Communion Outside of Mass.

While Communion is the logical completion of the Sacrifice of the Mass, with the participants partaking of the sacrifice they have just offered, the Church has not legislated that this is the only time when one can receive Communion. Even though some priests have acted as if it were an "either or" situation—either receive at Mass or not receive at all, the document, "Holy Communion and Worship of the Eucharist Outside of Mass", has clarified this point.

"It is better whenever possible to receive communion while participating at Mass, but the priest should not refuse to give communion if it is asked for outside of Mass. Indeed if anyone is prevented from joining the community at Mass, it is only right for him to have communion in private. This unites him with the eucharistic sacrifice and assures him of the loving support of the eucharistic community" (n. 14).

The actual rite for offering Holy Communion outside of Mass is like a Liturgy of the Word at Mass, with distribution of Communion added to it. There is a greeting, penitential rite, reading from Scripture, recitation of the Lord's Prayer, sign of peace, all the usual preparatory prayers for and during Communion as at Mass, a period of silent prayer or song, a concluding prayer, and blessing.

(If anyone but the priest or deacon is authorized to give out Communion, that person invokes God's blessing in a way different than the priest or deacon, and crosses himself or herself.) It would be appropriate if the service ended with a suitable hymn.

This simple Communion service replaces the all too brief service often conducted at Churches prior to the document. It could follow a devotional service. Since such a service would already include the Liturgy of the Word, it would begin with the Our Father.

EUCHARISTIC DEVOTIONS

SOME PRAYERS FROM THE LITURGY: (THE SACRAMENTARY):

Let us pray:
  (to the Lord who gives himself
    in the eucharist,
  that this sacrament may bring us
    salvation
  and peace)
Lord Jesus Christ,
you gave us the eucharist
as the memorial of your suffering
  and death.
May our worship of this sacrament
  of your body and blood
help us to experience the salvation
  you won for us
and the peace of the kingdom
where you live with the Father and
  the Holy Spirit,
one God, for ever and ever. Amen.

  (Sacramentary, Solemnity of Corpus Christi.)

Let us pray:
  (for the willingness to make present
     in our world
  the love of Christ shown to us in the
     eucharist)

Lord Jesus Christ,
we worship you living among us
in the sacrament of your body and blood.
May we offer to our Father in heaven
a solemn pledge of undivided love.
May we offer to our brothers and sisters
a life poured out in loving service of
   that kingdom
where you live with the Father and
   the Holy Spirit,
one God, for ever and ever. Amen.

(Sacramentary, Solemnity of Corpus Christi,
          Alternate Opening Prayer.)

Lord our God,
may we always give due honor
to the sacramental presence of the Lamb who
   was slain for us.
May our faith be rewarded
by the vision of his glory,
who lives and reigns for ever and ever.

            (Holy Communion and Worship of the
            Eucharist Outside of Mass,   225.)

PRAYER BEFORE COMMUNION

*Almighty and everlasting God, behold I come to
the Sacrament of Your only-begotten Son, our
Lord Jesus Christ: I come as one infirm to the phy-*

sician of life, as one unclean to the fountain of mercy, as one blind to the light of everlasting brightness, as one poor and needy to the Lord of heaven and earth.

Therefore, I implore the abundance of Your measureless bounty that You would heal my infirmity, wash my uncleanness, enlighten my blindness, enrich my poverty and clothe my nakedness, that I may receive the Bread of Angels, the King of kings, the Lord of lords, with such reverence and humility, with such sorrow and devotion, with such purity and faith, with such purpose and intention as may be profitable to my soul's salvation.

Grant to me, I pray, the grace of receiving not only the Sacrament of our Lord's Body and Blood, but also the grace and power of the Sacrament. O most gracious God, grant me so to receive the Body of Your only-begotten Son, our Lord Jesus Christ, which He took from the Virgin Mary, as to merit to be incorporated into His mystical Body, and to be numbered among His members.

O most loving Father, give me the grace to behold forever Your beloved Son with His face at last unveiled, whom I now intend to receive under the sacramental veil here below. Amen.

(The Raccolta, 158.)
(St. Thomas Aquinas c. 1225-1274)

EASTERN RITE PRAYER BEFORE COMMUNION

O Lord and Master Jesus Christ, my God, who alone has power to absolve men from their sins: forgive all my transgressions both deliberate and indeliberate, committed in word or deed. O Lover

93

of Mankind, allow me to partake of your divine, glorious, and pure Mysteries.

Let my sharing in your body and blood be for the cleansing of my sins and the healing of my body and a pledge of the life to come in your kingdom. You are a great God of mercy, loving and kind and full of compassion. To you I send up glory, Father, Son, and Holy Spirit. Amen.

(St. John of Damascus c. 690-749)

THANKSGIVING AFTER MASS

I give You thanks, holy Lord, Father almighty, everlasting God, who has fed me, a sinner, Your unworthy servant, for no merits of my own, but only out of the goodness of Your great mercy, with the precious Body and Blood of Your only-begotten Son, our Lord Jesus Christ; and I pray You, that this holy Communion may be to me, not guilt for punishment, but a saving intercession for pardon.

Let it be for me an armor of faith and a shield of good-will. Let it be to me a casting out of vices; a driving away of all evil desires and fleshy lusts; an increase of charity, patience, humility, obedience, and all other virtues; a firm defense against the plots of all my enemies, both seen and unseen; a perfect quieting of all motions of sin, both in my flesh and in my spirit; a firm cleaving unto You, the only and true God, and a happy ending of my life.

And I pray You to bring me, a sinner, to that ineffable Feast where You with Your Son and the Holy Spirit, are to Your holy ones true light, full *satisfaction, everlasting joy, consummate pleasure and perfect happiness. Amen.*

(The Raccolta,   161.)
(St. Thomas Aquinas c. 1225-1274)

EASTERN RITE PRAYER AFTER COMMUNION

We thank you, O Lord, and we ask you to make us worthy of this divine Communion, through which you forgive us, and help us begin a new and true Christian life in our families and Society, for the glory of your Holy Name, of your only-begotten Son and of your living and Holy Spirit. Amen.

O Lord God of Salvation, who became man for us and saved us by your immolation, save us from corruption that leads to damnation and make us a temple of your Holy Spirit, because by your choice and loving care, we are your faithful heir. To you be glory, honor, and power, together with your Father, and your living Holy Spirit, now and for ever. Amen.

(Anaphora of the Twelve Apostles, Maronite Rite.)

ANIMA CHRISTI: SOUL OF CHRIST

Soul of Christ, be my sanctification;
Body of Christ, be my salvation;
Blood of Christ, fill all my veins;
Water from Christ's side, wash out my stains;
Passion of Christ, my comfort be;
O good Jesus, listen to me;
In thy wounds I fain would hide;
Ne'er to be parted from thy side;

Guard me, should the foe assail me;
Call me when life shall fail me;
Bid me come to thee above;
With thy saints to sing thy love;
World without end. Amen.

(Translation: John Cardinal Newman)
(Partial Indulgence,   10.) *

SHORT PRAYERS TO JESUS IN THE EUCHARIST

Jesus, my God, I adore you here present
in the sacrament of your love!

O Sacrament most holy,
O Sacrament divine!
All praise and all thanksgiving
Be every moment thine!

(The Raccolta,   146,   136.)

DESIRE FOR THE EUCHARIST WHEN UNABLE TO RECEIVE (SPIRITUAL COMMUNION)

My Jesus, I believe .that you are present in the Blessed Sacrament, I love you above all things and I desire you in my soul. Since I cannot receive you now sacramentally, come at least spiritually into my soul. As though you were already there, I embrace you and unite myself wholly to you; permit not that I should ever be separated from you. Amen. (St. Alphonsus Liguori. 1696-1787.)

I believe that you, O Jesus, are in the Most Blessed Sacrament! I love you and desire you! Come into my heart. I embrace you. O never leave me! May the burning and most sweet power of your love, O Lord Jesus Christ, absorb my mind, that I may die through love of your love. who was pleased to die through love of my love.   Amen.

(St. Francis of Assisi, c. 1181-1226)

BYZANTINE RITE PRAYER TO THE EUCHARIST

It is indeed a tremendous miracle to see God taking flesh and becoming man, and a greater miracle still to see him suspended on the cross. But the highest of all miracles, O Christ our God, is your ineffable presence under the mystic species. Truly you did institute, through this Great Sacrament, a remembrance of all your marvels.   How merciful of you, O God, to give yourself as food to those who revere you. To recall our covenant forever, and to remember your passion and your death until the day of your glorious coming! Let us, O faithful, receive our food and our life, our King and our Savior, and cry out: "Save, O Lord, those who worship your glorious and venerable presence."

CONTEMPORARY PRAYER IN GRATITUDE FOR THE EUCHARIST

Loving and kind Father, we offer you praise and thanks for the gift of the Eucharist, which your only-begotten Son has given to us. This great sacrament   perfectly   signifies   and   wonderfully

97

brings about a sharing in the life of the Trinity as well as the unity of your people by which the Church exists. We acknowledge that the Eucharist is the summit of both the action by which you sanctify the world and of the worship which men offer to you through our Lord Jesus Christ. Together with him, we the Church perform the role of priest and victim, and offer to you, our heavenly Father, a total offering of Christ and ourselves for our own salvation and that of the whole world.

Aid us, our good Father, with the strength of this sacramental food to live joyfully and gratefully, ever sharing in the death and resurrection of Christ, your Son and our Brother. May it help us to do good works, live a life pleasing to you, be devoted to the Church, and fill the world with your Spirit, as we serve you as your faithful witness in all things, in the midst of human affairs. This we ask in Christ's name in the midst of the Church. Amen.

(After the Constitution on the Sacred Liturgy and Instruction on the Eucharistic Mystery.)

CONTEMPORARY PRAYER IN HONOR OF THE EUCHARIST

Lord Jesus Christ, our eternal High Priest and infinitely-perfect Victim for the salvation of humankind, we thank you for making the Eucharistic Sacrifice of your Body and Blood our means for remembering your death and resurrection and of perpetuating and representing the Sacrifice of the Cross in an unbloody manner. By means of the Mystery of the Eucharist that which was offered once on Calvary is marvelously re-enacted and its saving power is constantly recalled and applied for the salvation of the whole world.

As we continually repeat that same sacrifice, you call us to take part more fully in the celebration of the Eucharist by eating of the paschal banquet, sacramental Communion. May it be for us, your faithful followers, a sacrament of devotion, a sign of unity, a bond of charity, a holy meal in which you are received, the soul filled with grace, and a pledge is given of future glory. Until we see you face to face at the eternal banquet in your Father's kingdom, we live and pray united through you, with you, and in you, in the unity of the Holy Spirit, for the glory and honor of the almighty Father, for ever and ever. Amen. Amen. Amen.

(After the *Constitution on the Sacred Liturgy* and the *Instruction on the Eucharistic Mystery*.)

PRAYER TO CHRIST AND HIS EUCHARISTIC HEART

Glory be to you, O Christ, true God and true Man, for you are the Lover of Mankind and Lamb of God who takes away the sins of the world. The Church has learned to honor and adore your person, especially under the aspect of your Eucharistic Heart. On the night on which you were betrayed, you instituted the Sacrament of your love. To pour out your riches on humankind, you not only immolated yourself on Calvary, but still offer yourself to the Father in eucharistic signs through the hands of the priest. You remain ceaselessly present among us in our tabernacles and desire to unite yourself to each one of us, and through us, with all men and women. In this great sacrament, O Lord, your Eucharistic Heart beats with sacrificial and joyous love for the Father and for the whole wide world.

The Church is grateful that she was born of your pierced Heart and is a community of love. By ceaselessly receiving your Body and Blood, the Church perfects her members and seeks the grace to continue your mission of service to be ever grateful for this redemptive love. Guide us, Lord and Brother, in our life of discipleship until we love everyone as you have loved us.

For all glory, honor, worship and love are due through you to the Father, in the unity of the Holy Spirit, now and always and for ever and ever. Amen.

THE DIVINE PRAISES

Blessed be God.

Blessed be His Holy Name.

Blessed be Jesus Christ, True God and True Man.

Blessed be the Name of Jesus.

Blessed be His Most Sacred Heart.

Blessed be His Most Precious Blood.

Blessed be Jesus in the Most Holy Sacrament.

Blessed be the Holy Spirit, the Paraclete.

Blessed be the great Mother of God.

Blessed be her holy and Immaculate Conception.

Blessed be her glorious Assumption.

Blessed be the name of Mary, Virgin and Mother.

Blessed be Saint Joseph, her most chaste Spouse.
Blessed be God in His Angels and in His Saints.

TO OUR LADY OF THE BLESSED SACRAMENT

O Virgin Mary, our Lady of the Blessed Sacrament, you are the glory of the Christian people, joy of the universal Church, salvation of the whole world. Pray for us, and awaken in all believers a lively devotion to the Most Holy Eucharist, so that they may be made worthy to partake of the same daily. Amen.

(The Raccolta,   418.)

A partial indulgence may be gained whenever one visits the Blessed Sacrament to adore It. A plenary indulgence may be gained if the visit lasts for at least half an hour. (Grant   13.)

SCRIPTURE READINGS SUITABLE FOR EUCHARISTIC DEVOTIONS

Gen. 14: 18-20   Mk. 14: 12-26
Ex. 16: 2-4, 12-15   Jn. 19: 31-37
Ex. 24: 3-8   Lk. 9: 11-17
Acts 2: 42-47   Jn. 6: 1-15
Acts 10: 34-43   Jn. 6: 24-35
1 Cor. 10: 16-17   Jn. 6: 41-51
1 Cor. 11: 23-26   Jn. 6: 51-58
            Ps. 23
            Ps. 34
            Ps. 116: 12-18
            Ps. 145: 10-18

HERE, LORD JESUS,
YOU ARE BOTH SHEPHERD
AND GREEN PASTURE.

(St. Thomas Aquinas, c. 1225-1274.)

5

DAILY
OFFERING

A DAILY OFFERING PRAYER

Eternal Father,
I offer you everything I do this day:
my work, my prayers, my apostolic efforts;
my time with family and friends;
my hours of relaxation;
my difficulties, problems, distress,
which I shall try to bear with patience.

Join these, my gifts,
to the unique offering
which Jesus Christ, your Son,
renews today in the Eucharist.

Grant, I pray,
that, vivified by the Holy Spirit
and united to the Sacred Heart of Jesus,
my life this day may be of service
to you and to your children
and help consecrate the world to you.
Amen.

APOSTLESHIP OF PRAYER
114 East 13th St., New York, N.Y. 10003
With Ecclesiastical Approval

No. 202

When love letters are published, it is amazing how complete is the gift of the lover to the beloved. The Morning or Daily Offering was devised as a practical answer to Christ's request to St. Margaret Mary Alacoque (1673-1675) for the love of mankind. For well over a century and a quarter this little prayer has been one of the most durable and widely used devotional practices in the Church. Like love letters, the Morning or Daily Offering tells Jesus that we love him so much that we give him all.

HISTORY OF THE OFFERING PRAYER

Around the year 1844, a Jesuit teacher, Rev. Francis X. Gaulrelet, decided to harness the enthusiasm, prayers, and activities of his young students with a daily offering prayer. He did it with Christ's loving request to St. Margaret Mary Alacoque in mind, and it worked. In 1860, he merged his group with the League of the Sacred Heart. This new union popularized the saying of the Morning Offering through the pages of its magazine, *The Messenger of the Sacred Heart.*

In just a few years, there were millions of people praying the Morning Offering at the start of the day. With the advent of the "Monthly Leaflet", zealously promoted by parish priests and teaching Sisters, the prayer spread even more widely. The prayer has continued to keep its popularity—whenever it is properly explained and copies of it are made available for immediate use.

THE PURPOSE OF THE PRAYER

Since Christ asked for our love in the pages of Scripture—and he merely repeated this perennial request in his message to St. Margaret Mary Alacoque, many people find it useful to have some practical means to carry out their response to this request for love. While it is true that one can make up a new "Morning Offering" every day, many people find that they are not so sharp or creative that early in the morning.

No doubt some people are, but many, many people seek some aid to help them consecrate themselves and their day to Christ and to the service of their neighbor. Such an aid has been the Morning or Daily Offering printed by the Apostleship of Prayer. When it is pasted on the bathroom mirror, people splash their faces with water, look up, and there is the reminder to offer their day to Christ.

106

It is so simple and so practical! Its *enduring value* is precisely in the desire of everyone to respond to Christ's call for love, beginning with our good intention. That little prayer is the initial step in loving—a prayer suitable even for sleepy beginnings! After saying a prayer of words, they spend the rest of the day living a prayer of action. What they have promised in words, they carry out in loving service to God and his loved ones.

RELATION TO THE LITURGY

Long before the Second Vatican Council—in fact since its own very early days, the Morning or Daily Offering united the "prayers, works, joys and sufferings" of one's life to the offering of Christ in the Mass. While their understanding of the Mass certainly deepened with the Council, those who used the Offering Prayer were reassured that what they had been doing for so long was "relevant".

When the *Dogmatic Constitution on the Church* in Section 34, paralleled the ideas in the Morning or Daily Offering, such users saw the Offering Prayer paraphrased—intentionally or not—in those sentences. It reads: "For all their works, prayers, and apostolic endeavors, their ordinary married and family life, their daily labors, their mental and physical relaxation, if carried out in the Spirit, and even the hardships of life, if patiently borne—all of these become spiritual sacrifices acceptable to God through Jesus Christ (cf. 1 Peter 2: 5).

"During the celebration of the Eucharist, these

sacrifices are most lovingly offered to the Father along with the Lord's body. Thus, as worshippers whose every deed is holy, the laity consecrate the world itself to God." The Council, then, told them that what they had been doing "in union with the Holy Sacrifice of the Mass throughout the world" was the right way to pray and to live.

UPDATING THE OFFERING PRAYER

First, those who used the Morning or Daily offering Prayer should more consciously unite their lives to the Eucharistic liturgy. "The liturgy is the summit towards which the activity of the Church is directed; at the same time it is the font from which all her powers flow" (*Constitution on the Sacred Liturgy,* n. 10). True as that is, so many of the faithful do not celebrate the liturgy—either by habit or circumstances—more often than once a week. Hence, it is everyone's challenge to make the liturgy effective and alive from celebration to celebration, from weekend to weekend.

While it is true that the words of the Offering Prayer directs our "prayers, works, joys, and sufferings" to the Mass, one has to continually work (against the effects of habit) to mean every word that one is saying. One might even like to use an alternate form of the Offering Prayer from time to time to help in this resolution. But, it still comes back to the same challenge—continual effort to mean what one is saying.

Second, the Offering Prayer should be deeply rooted in the communal aspect of the Church. The Church is the community of those who love Christ and live according to that belief. The doctrine of the Communion of Saints, the Mystical Body, and the People of God push back the limits of our imagination and concern to include all those who are united to Christ by baptism and any degree of faith and love.

Instead of a narrow "me and God spirituality", those beliefs lead us to a way of life which is communitarian: "in Christ with us together". While few would deny this, everyone has the problem of getting so involved in the details of life that we tend to overlook it.

The Morning or Daily Offering is offered "for all the intentions of our Holy Father", because he is the "permanent and visible source and foundation of unity and fellowship" (*Dogmatic Constitution on the Church,* n. 18). It is he who reveals to us the needs of the Church Universal, as well as those of all men of good will.

Through the Monthly Leaflet published by the Apostleship of Prayer, his monthly and mission intentions are made known to the faithful. These intentions should be seen not only as prayer objectives, but also possible work objectives. United with Christ our Head, we the members of His body must work and pray for those things which he does have at Heart. The surest sign of our sincerity in praying the Daily Offering is the transfer of the words of prayer into Christian actions.

Third, one could gradually change his or her

practice of saying the Morning Offering in the morning only, and see it as a Daily Offering to be renewed many times during the day—at least, morning, noon, and evening. As the ordinary day progresses, we tend to remember less and less what we planned or intended to do in the morning.

The renewal of the offering would be very useful to keep up the momentum of our intentions. While the use of a prayer formula is not necessary, some conscious attempt should be made to renew the self-offering involved. The Saints recommended either wordless prayers or short ones, which used to be called "aspirations". An example of such a prayer would be: "All for you, most Sacred Heart of Jesus".

Fourth, one could ask the intercession of the Blessed Virgin Mary to add her love and intercession to our offering. Mother of the Church and model of the perfect Christian that she is, she can show us in her example how a sincere Christian hears the word of God and keeps it (Luke 8: 21). The last three popes (Pius XII, John XXIII, and Paul VI) have recommended that we pray to Mary under the title of the Immaculate Heart of Mary.

As with devotion to the Heart of Jesus, the heart is seen as the totality of the person and center of her loving relationship to God and with others. By praying in this way, we ask the deepest and most wonderful part of the Virgin Mother to become part of our "prayers, works, joys, and sufferings", so that it is most pleasing to Almighty God.

All of these considerations are part of the thrust

of the Apostleship of Prayer. This organization is an international movement, without meetings or dues, which popularizes the total giving of self to God through the medium of the Daily Offering prayer and motivates this dedication through devotion to the Heart of Jesus.

The prayer verbalizes our intention to unite all that we are and do to the daily Masses celebrated all over the world, but especially in our own local church. It encourages a way of life involving deep love of Christ and those things which he has at Heart, love of his Mother (through daily Marian prayer, especially part or all of the rosary), and love of the Church (through prayer for and cooperation to achieve the monthly and mission intentions of our Holy Father, the Pope).

(You can learn about the Apostleship of Prayer, the Monthly Leaflets, and the *Messenger of the Sacred Heart* from your pastor, since each pastor is the local director of the Apostleship in his parish. Many dioceses also have a diocesan director to assist in understanding and living the twenty-four hour a day spirituality of the Apostleship of Prayer. Since the Jesuits—the Society of Jesus—have spearheaded the promotion of devotion to the Heart of Jesus and the Apostleship of Prayer, their members could also be contacted for assistance in promoting and practicing this devotion.)

MORNING AND NIGHT PRAYERS

PRAYERS FROM THE LITURGY OF HOURS:

Almighty Father,
you have brought us to the light of a new day;
keep us safe the whole day through
from every sinful inclination.
May all our thoughts, words and actions
aim at doing what is pleasing in your sight.
We ask this through our Lord Jesus Christ, your
Son,
who lives and reigns with you and the Holy Spirit,
one God, for ever and ever.

   (Monday, Morning Prayer, Week II.)

(During the day.)

Father, may everything we do
begin with your inspiration
and continue with your saving help.
Let our work find its origin in you
and through you reach completion.
We ask this .... (above).

   (Monday, Daytime Prayer, Week II.)

(Night Prayer)

Almighty Father,
you have given us the strength
to work throughout this day.
Receive our evening sacrifice of praise
in thanksgiving for your countless gifts.
We ask this .... (above).

(Monday, Evening Prayers, Week II.)

TRADITIONAL MORNING/DAILY OFFERING PRAYER:

Jesus, through the Immaculate Heart of Mary,
I offer You all my prayers, works, joys, and
sufferings of this day,
in union with the Holy Sacrifice of the Mass
throughout the world.
I offer them for all the intentions of Your Sacred
Heart:
the salvation of souls, reparation for sins,
the reunion of all Christians.
I offer them for the intentions of our Bishops
and of all members of the Apostleship of Prayer,
and in particular for those recommended
by our Holy Father this month. Amen.

(USA and Canadian Apostleship of Prayer.)

CONTEMPORARY OFFERING PRAYER:

Eternal Father, I offer You everything I do
this day:
my work, my prayers, my apostolic efforts;

113

my time with family and friends; my hours of
relaxation;
my difficulties, problems, distresses
which I shall try to bear with patience.
Join these my gifts to the unique offering
which Jesus Christ, your Son, renews today in
the Eucharist.
Grant, I pray, that vivified by the Holy Spirit
and united to the Sacred Heart of Jesus
and the Immaculate Heart of Mary,
my life this day may be of service to You and
to your children
and help consecrate the world to You. Amen.

(USA and Canadian Apostleship of Prayer.)

AN ECUMENICAL OFFERING PRAYER:

My God, I offer you this day
all that I shall think or do or say,
uniting it with what was done on earth
by Jesus Christ, your Son. Amen.

EASTERN RITE MORNING PRAYER:

O Master and holy God, who surpass understanding, at whose word light came forth out of
darkness, who in your mercy gives us rest through
night-long sleep and raised us up to glorify your
goodness and offer our supplication to You: now
also in your tender love accept us who adore
You and give thanks to You with all our hearts.
Grant us all our requests if they lead to salvation; give us the grace of manifesting that we
are sons of light and heirs of your eternal rewards.

114

In the abundance of your mercies, O Lord, remember all your people: all those present here who pray with us, all our brethren on land or at sea, in every place of your domain, who call upon your love for men: upon them all pour down your great mercy, that we, saved in body and soul, may persevere unfailingly and that, in our confidence, we may magnify your exalted and blessed name, Father, Son, and Holy Spirit, now and always and for ever and ever. Amen.

(Matins, Fourth Morning Prayer. Byzantine Rite.)

TRADITIONAL NIGHT PRAYER:

I adore You, O God,
and I love You with all my heart.
I give You thanks for having created me,
for having made me a Christian,
and for having preserved me this day.
Pardon me for the evil I have done today;
if I have done anything good, accept it.
Keep me while I take my rest
and deliver me from all dangers.
May your grace be always with me. Amen.

(The Raccolta, 53.)

CONTEMPORARY NIGHT PRAYER:

O God my Father, now that this day is over, I turn to you once again in prayer. I thank you for the good that you have helped me to accomplish as your partner. I am sorry for my sins and faults, because they have offended you, hurt others, and prevented you from doing more through me. I praise you for all the gifts you have given to me and to everyone this day. Bless those I love or who have been good to me.

Grant a refreshing sleep to everyone who goes to bed this night. Give health and energy to those who rise to the light of a new day. Encourage those pressed down by injustices, console those whose hearts are heavy with sadness, help us to nourish those who hunger and thirst for the things of the body and of the soul. Bless the Church and those who dedicate their lives to your service. May all peoples praise and thank you continually. As I unite this prayer to all the Masses being celebrated around the world, may I be guided by the Heart of Jesus, in the love of the Holy Spirit, until I reach my heavenly home with you and with all your children for ever and ever.

Mary, Woman of faith and my own dear Mother, along with my Guardian Angel and Patron Saints, join your prayers to mine as I end this day praising and loving the Father, the Son, and the Holy Spirit now and always. Amen.

NIGHT PRAYER FROM THE EASTERN RITE:

O Great and Wonderful God, who pursues all things with ineffable love and universal providence, who created all things in wisdom, dividing light from darkness, setting up the sun to govern the day, the moon and stars to rule the night, who provides for us with the bounties of this world and assures us of obtaining the promised kingdom: You have made us worthy to reach this hour and to come into your presence with our thanks and to offer You our evening praise. O Lord and Lover of Mankind, grant that this coming night may be spent in peace; forgive us our sins and those of your people through the intercession of the Mother of God; and give us the grace to rise refreshed to sing your praise, O You the only Gracious One and Lover of Mankind.

For You are our God and we send up our glory to You, Father, Son, and Holy Spirit, now and always and for ever and ever. Amen.

(Office of Vespers, Sixth and Seventh Prayer. Byzantine Rite.)

SHORT PRAYERS:

Into your hands, O Lord, I commend my spirit.
(Ps. 30:6)

Jesus, I live for you;
Jesus, I die for you;
Jesus, I am yours in life and in death.
Amen.

All for you, Most Sacred Heart of Jesus.

SCRIPTURE READINGS FOR SERVICES OF DEDICATION

Jos. 24:1-2, 15-25	Rom. 6:3-11
Is. 44:1-11	Gal. 4:4-7
Is. 44:1-11	Gal. 5:16-25

Eph. 1:3-14   Mt. 25:14-30

Eph. 4:1-4   Jn. 7:37-39

Titus 3:4-7   Jn. 14:15-17

I Peter 2:4-10   Jn. 15:1-11

Mt. 16:2-27

Ps. 1

Ps. 23

Ps. 96

Ps. 138

Ps. 145

WHATEVER YOU DO,

OFFER IT UP TO GOD,

AND PRAY THAT IT MAY BE

FOR HIS HONOR AND GLORY.

(St. Teresa of Avila, 1515-1592.)

6

THE
BLESSED
VIRGIN

During the closing days of the II Vatican Council, many things happened so quickly that their significance was only appreciated later. One such day was November 21, 1964. The first important thing which happened was the solemn issuing of the great conciliar document, *The Dogmatic Constitution on the Church*. [This document ends with the beautiful chapter (VIII) entitled, "The Role of the Blessed Virgin, Mother of God, in the Mystery of the Church".]

The second important occurrence came as a surprise to the assembled bishops: Pope Paul VI said, "I proclaim Our Lady, Mother of the Church". While the Council came close to saying that in one section of the document (n. 55), the Pope said it very explicitly.

He immediately followed this statement with the third important thing which happened that day. "Our glance opens on the endless horizons of the entire world," he said, "the object of the most lively care of the Ecumenical Council and which our venerated predecessor, Pius XII, of venerable memory, *not without inspiration from on high* (italics mine), solemnly consecrated to the Immaculate Heart of Mary. Today we consider it particularly opportune to renew this act of consecration."

The world press picked up the first and second of these happenings, but missed the third. The Bishop of Fatima registered his feelings about these things in the words, "With all the other bishops I was immobilized in cope and miter, but inwardly I leaped."

He correctly analyzed the significance of the last words as he explained in these words, "What struck me most was that the Holy Father should introduce a private revelation into the Council." That the Holy Father meant exactly what the Bishop of Fatima and other bishops there present thought he meant we learn from his encyclical, *The Great Sign* (May 13, 1967), in which he wrote, "We ourselves renewed this consecration of Pope Pius XII on November 21, 1964".

In the following pages, one chapter will be devoted to explaining devotion to Our Lady in general, and a second one on the Rosary.

VENERATION VS. ADORATION

True or orthodox Catholic doctrine on the Blessed Virgin maintains that there is a vast difference between the honor paid to God and that which is offered to the Virgin Mary and the Saints.

The words "adoration" and "worship", in the truest sense of these words, can only be rendered to God. These words mean that we acknowledge only God as the Supreme Being, Ground of all things, ultimate Source of natural and supernatural life, the Conserver, the Lord, and the eventual Judge of all. While they are not always used with precision in modern writing, the words of Deuteronomy (6: 13) express it well, "You shall do homage to the Lord your God; him alone shall you adore".

The honor or respect which is given to Mary and the Saints is, obviously, far below this! That is why the word "veneration" is used of this honor in Catholic writings. This honor is offered to them *because of their relationship to God.* They are his friends. They have received the gifts of his grace in faith and thanksgiving, have cooperated with them to the fullest, and are now living happily in his presence forever as his special friends.

While God offers his love to everyone, some make his will and response to his love the center of their lives; others make it only one of many things they are concerned about during their lifetime. Because of their special relationship with God, the Saints love us in God and desire to help us to achieve that same happy end. In the Communion of Saints, love transcends earth, heaven and purgatory and desires to love and help people everywhere: "Love never ends" (1 Cor. 13: 8).

Since we have been called by God to assist each other on our pilgrim way to the Father's home, this must be seen as compatible with the sole mediatorship of Christ (1 Tim. 2: 5). In cooperation with Christ, by God's free choice, this assistance to each other is part of the message of Christian love. The Virgin and Saints do not love us less in their possession of the God of love, but more! And it is upon this belief that the Catholic doctrine of the intercession rests!

ORIGIN OF FEAST DAYS

Originally, the early Church celebrated only one feastday, and that was the weekly commemoration of the Lord's Resurrection each Sunday. In the course of time, the Church added annual feasts to remember the day on which a martyr gave us his or her life out of love of Christ. In a very real way they imitated the death of Christ in their lives and God glorified them with life with him forever.

When the persecutions ended after about three centuries, the Church saw another type of martyrdom and identification with Christ as holy virgins, hermits, and others controlled the impulses of nature, lived heroic lives of virtue and service to others. This early veneration of the martyrs, Saints and the Virgin Mary was always subordinated to that fact that, after the Incarnation and Redemption, everything comes from God through Christ and is handed over to his lordship.

Yet, even in this supreme mediatorship and lordship, God left us a very real duty to love one another and help one another in Christ. To all our loving efforts, Christ adds his own great love and hands it over to the Father. Whether we are conscious of it or not, all things flow to the Father

124

through him; we simply add our small efforts to the all-powerful love of his Heart as he continually intercedes for us before the Father.

During the doctrinal controversies on the nature of Christ which raged during the 5th and 6th Centuries, this perfect balance in attitude and practice in the popular mind was upset. The more the divinity of Jesus was strongly stated to counteract the heresies at that time, the more distant the humanity and mediatorship of Christ felt to the ordinary person.

This led to difficulties in imagining one's relationship to this distant "go between" (Mediator) with the Father and themselves. To narrow the distance, the less educated soon visualized the possibility of the Blessed Virgin standing between her Son and themselves. In time, some even felt that the Sinless One was too good to bother often with them, so they envisioned the Saints between themselves and Mary.

This hierarchy of intercessors showed the firm belief these people had in the love and concern of Mary and the Saints for them, but it was a poor way to explain orthodox doctrine! In such a climate, the people asked for more and more feasts of Saints and participated less and less in the actual prayers and singing of the Mass. With the altar at the far end of the church against the wall, and priest turned to face it, the Eucharistic celebration appeared as a sacred drama to be watched as one said his or her own private prayers—which included many to the Blessed Virgin and Saints.

With poor liturgical forethought, Church officials granted many such requests. As feastdays piled up, some even on Sunday, the weekly commemoration of the Resurrection did not stand out in the sharpness which it should have. The veneration of the Saints, at least in some places, did appear to make up a major part of the spiritual life of the ordinary people. When the Reformation came along, the Reformers did not correct the situation as much as simply do away with the veneration of the Saints. Yet, the doctrine underlying the practice is intimately tied to the message of unending love which the Risen Lord asks of all, even the glorified Christians in heaven.

THE COUNCIL AND MARY

The II Vatican Council, like many other Ecumenical Councils before it, incorporated many sentences from preceding councils to give a summary of the Church's traditional teaching before adding its own insights.

In Chapter VIII of the *Dogmatic Constitution on the Church,* the II Vatican Council speaks of the Blessed Mary's Immaculate Conception, perpetual virginity, divine and spiritual motherhood, her Assumption, her powerful role within the mediatorship of her Son, and so forth. The Council brought out in a special way that Mary was a woman of faith, of great service to her Son, the perfect example of a follower of Christ, etc.

In addition to this document, the American bishops issued a consideration of the Virgin Mother under the title of *Behold Your Mother, Woman of Faith* (1973). Pope Paul VI wrote an Apostolic Exhortation, *Marian Devotions* (1974), to urge devotion to the Mother of God, as well as explain some principles for renewing devotion to her. He spent a good deal of space discussing the example which the liturgy offered to us in our devotions to Mary.

SPIRITUAL MOTHERHOOD AND MEDIATION

Since God the Father freely chose Mary to be of service to mankind's redemption and Christ took flesh of his Mother, it was very natural to honor so chosen a person as Mary. The touching scene in John's account (19: 25-27) in which Jesus said, "Son, behold your mother", has led many Christians to believe in Mary's concern for them as a legitimate expression of her spiritual motherhood.

The American bishops (in the document cited above, n. 71) propose such a spiritual motherhood from other words in the Bible. Jesus taught that anyone who heard the word of God and lived it was mother, and brother, and sister to him (Mt. 12: 50). If anyone can achieve such a relationship to Jesus, how much more so "the perfect example" of such love and fidelity? It is hardly thinkable that her loving interest so clearly evident in the incident of the wedding feast at Cana (Jn. 2: 1-12) would be any less now in heavenly clarity.

Roman Catholics, Orthodox Christians and some Protestants see intercession as a logical and necessary conclusion of such biblical thinking. In Christ's all-powerful mediatorship with the Father, there is still room for the loving concern of one for another. Since we do help one another on earth by our prayers and assistance, the Church sees and teaches that this concern does not end with death. It continues as Mary and the Saints join their prayers to ours as we call upon God in our need and joy.

ENDURING VALUE OF DEVOTION TO MARY

No doubt much devotion to Mary rises from memories of the love and concern of one's own mother. Most of us have experienced the responsive hand of a friend when one was in need. If such enriching feelings flow from our human love, how much more valid is the love of Jesus' Mother for his disciples in their efforts to be Christ-like? After all, his loving Heart responded to her urgings even though his hour had not yet come (Jn. 2: 4).

People call upon the Mother to seek her prayers and help. The countless products of art in her honor, the thousands of churches erected under her name, the reams of parchment and paper extolling her love, the votive offerings given in thanksgiving at hundreds of shrines, the lives of service motivated by her example tell of the obvious enduring value of this devotion. In a special way it is to be found in the liturgy of all rites of the Church.

RELATIONSHIP TO THE LITURGY

Pope Paul VI offered the liturgy itself as the best teacher of the Church's attitude towards devotion to the Blessed Virgin Mary. He called it "the golden norm for Christian piety". "From the perennial tradition kept alive by reason of the uninterrupted presence of the Spirit and continual attention to the Word, the Church of our times draws motives, arguments and incentives for the veneration that she pays the Blessed Virgin. And the liturgy, which receives approval and strength from the Magisterium, is a most lofty expression and an evident form of this living tradition" (*Marian Devotions,* n. 15).

While the Pope spent a good deal of time describing the liturgy of the Roman Rite, the same trait is true of all rites. The Eastern Rites especially are warm and abundant in their prayers to Mary. (In the Byzantine Rite, for instance, well over a dozen references will be found to Mary in the Sacred Liturgy.) The same is also true of the Orthodox Churches.

In each of the Eucharistic Prayers one finds these prayers to Mary. One finds it in Penitential Rite I, the Nicene Creed, two ordinary Prefaces to the Virgin Mary (I and II), special Prefaces for the Immaculate Conception and Assumption in the Preface of St. Joseph, for Weekday IV, and so on.

We also find this liturgical devotion in those feasts of Mary kept by the Universal Church. They have been reduced in number after the II Vatican Council—not for lack of devotion, but rather to make the days of the Lord more Solemn, open up more days for weekday and theme Masses, and allow local calendars to select those feasts which are truly of local character.

The official Roman Calendar lists the following Marian celebrations: The Solemnity of Mary, Mother of God (Jan. 1); Our Lady of Lourdes, Memorial (Feb. 11); The Annunciation, Solemnity (Mar. 25); The Visitation, Feast (May 31); Immaculate Heart of Mary (on the Saturday following the Solemnity of the Sacred Heart), Memorial; Our Lady of Mount Carmel, Memorial (July 16).

Then there is the Dedication of St. Mary Major Basilica, Memorial (Aug. 5); the Assumption, Solemnity (Aug. 15); The Queenship of Mary, Memorial (Aug. 22); the Birth of Mary, Feast (Sept. 8); Our Lady of Sorrows, Memorial (Sept. 15); Our Lady of the Rosary, Memorial (Oct. 7); the Presentation of Mary, Memorial (Nov. 21); the Immaculate Conception, Solemnity (Dec. 8); (in the United States, Our Lady of Guadalupe, Memorial on Dec. 12); and the Holy Family, Feast (on the Sunday within the octave of Christmas or on Dec. 30 if there is no such Sunday).

The present rubrics or directives for the celebrant allows for a Votive Mass of the Blessed Virgin on Saturdays which are open, as well as on open weekdays. The liturgy provides three Common Masses of the Virgin Mary, a seasonal Mass for Advent, Christmas, and Easter, and dozens of Scripture readings to make sure that the celebrations in honor of Mary harmonize with the liturgical seasons. These same books, the Sacramentary and Lectionary, should provide selections to make paraliturgical prayer also harmonize with the liturgical seasons. (Cfr. selection given below.)

If you have a church calendar, circle all of the Marian Feasts so that you can observe them in a special way. If you do not have such a calendar, copy the names of all the Marian Feasts on page 130 on your regular calendar.

HOW MUCH DEVOTION IS ENOUGH?

To a person who loves a husband or wife, the question never arises how much love is enough? One simply loves as much as one can! It is hard to answer the question: how much devotion is enough? One will answer that query according to the degree of love he or she *feels* for the Blessed Virgin.

Certainly one does love the Mother of God by full participation in the liturgy and the use of the Hail Mary in prayer. Some, though, will feel a greater attraction to Marian devotions, with varying degrees of emotional involvement. "A middle course is recommended between extremes of too much and too little," urge the American bishops in *Behold Your Mother* (n. 91).

Pope John XXIII and Pope Paul VI warn the faithful to avoid exaggerated writings and devotions to Our Lady without specifying exactly which ones are meant. "This most holy Synod...," we read in the *Dogmatic Constitution on the Church,* "admonishes all the sons of the Church that the cult, especially the liturgical cult, of the Blessed Virgin, be generously fostered. It charges that practices and exercises of devotion towards her be treasured as recommended by the teaching authority of the Church in the course of centuries, and that those decrees issued in earlier times regarding the veneration of images of Christ, the Blessed Virgin, and the saints, be religiously observed".

It continued: "in treating the unique dignity of the Mother of God, (they should) carefully and equally avoid the falsity of exaggeration on the one hand and the excess of narrow-mindedness on the other" (n. 67). Perhaps, to conclude the matter, the wise words remembered by John Cardinal Newman in the 19th Century of Rev. E. B. Pusey are still the best: "He said that we could not love the Blessed Virgin too much, if we love Our Lord a great deal more".

UPDATING MARIAN DEVOTIONS

First, we should always use the liturgy as a guide. Not only can we insert prayers from the Sacramentary into these devotions, but we can write prayers after the liturgical models. These prayers are careful to recognize that one should praise and thank God for his graces to Mary, pledge imitation of her loving and continual cooperation with those graces—which resulted in the virtues which we admire in her life, and, then, ask her intercession.

Perhaps, the "give me, give me, give me" attitude of some people's prayer betrays a poor understanding and living of the Church's teaching on Mary, rather than the deep trust they profess to have in her. One should proceed from praise and thanks to imitation and petition.

In Pope Paul's Apostolic Exhortation, *Marian Devotions* (n. 24-39), he outlines the Trinitarian, Christological, ecclesial, ecumenical, biblical, liturgical, and anthropological basis for the principles of renewal discussed in Chapter Two of this book. They are to be applied to devotions "for a renewal that will permit them to substitute elements that are transient, to emphasize the elements that are ever new and to incorporate that doctrinal data obtained from theological reflection and the proposals of the Church's Magisterium" (op. cit., n. 24).

Second, meaningful ancient practices should be left unchanged, but used with the proper attitudes of praise and thanksgiving to God, pledge of imitation of Mary, and, then, broad Christian concern for others as well as self. Among these ancient prayers would be: (1) the Hail Mary (Ave Maria); (2) the Hail Holy Queen (Salve, Regina); (3) the Memorare; and (4) the Angelus.

The Hail Mary. This prayer is made up of the New Testament quotations from Luke's account, first of the words of the angel (1: 28)—"Hail Mary, full of grace, the Lord is with you; blessed are you among women", and those of Elizabeth (1: 42)—"blessed is the fruit of your womb". Both were used singly since ancient times as antiphons in the Liturgy of Hours. Then they were joined as one antiphon. As the Little Office of the Blessed Virgin spread in countless Books of Hours, the words were used as a separate little devotional prayer. The "primitive Hail Mary" developed during the 11th Century. In the 13th Century, the word "Jesus" was added.

Still later in the 14th Century several versions of the last part of the prayer gradually developed until we have the present words, "Holy Mary, Mother of God, pray for us sinners, now and at the hour of our death. Amen". Since the first half comes from Luke, Pope Paul called the Hail Mary a "Gospel Prayer"—especially when one uses the meditations which rise out of the Gospel passages while praying them.

Hail Holy Queen; Memorare. (The text of these prayers will be found in the Prayer Section at the end of this chapter.) The Hail Holy Queen was composed by an unknown author of the 11th Century. It is traditionally sung or said as the final prayer of the day in the Liturgy of the Hours at the Hour of Compline. It is also known by its latin title, *Salve Regina.* It is a prayer of trust in the mercy obtained by the prayers of Mary for her children. The *Memorare* is said to be written by St. Bernard of Clairvaux (d. 1153). It is a shorter prayer of loving trust.

The Angelus. (Text below.) At one time, when church bells rang at 6:00 A.M., 12:00 noon, and 6:00 P.M. it was not merely to indicate the time of day, but also to remind people to say the Angelus. In the days when only the church, town hall, and castle had clocks, it is not surprising that prayer was linked with the ringing of bells in the community.

Already in the 13th Century, the Hail Mary was said at the ringing of bells, but the Angelus reached its present form during the 16th Century. It became customary to recall the Incarnation at the ringing of the bells and to pray in gratitude and praise, with a final general petition to make the passion and resurrection of Christ active in one's life.

Pope Paul urged the readoption of this lovely custom in his Apostolic Exhortation, *Marian Devotions* (n. 41). Since everyone is so time conscious these days, it might be good to use this devotion to sanctify the passage of time—much like a priest or religious uses the Liturgy of the Hours.

Third, updating the scapular. The scapular was a medieval apron, which monks and nuns adopted as part of their religious outfit. People living near the monasteries and convents asked the monks' and nuns' prayers and were influenced by them in their Christian life. To allow these people some sense of "belonging" to their communities, the monks and nuns encouraged membership in their "Third Orders". (The First Order was for the male religious, and the Second for the female.) The long piece of cloth which hung down in front and back with hole in the center for the head—the scapular —became an outward sign of this affiliation.

In time, small scapulars developed, especially for those who did not wish to associate themselves in Third Orders, but still wished to imitate the spirit of a particular community and ask its prayers.

Pope Paul VI singled out the Scapular of Our Lady of Mount Carmel and the rosary as two Marian practices as being "recommended by the teaching authority of the Church in the course of the centuries" (*Dogmatic Constitution on the Church,* n. 67).

Those who have problems in accepting the relevance of medals and scapulars have only to consider the peace signs and American flags of the 1960's, the ecology symbols of the 1970's, and the wide use of the cross especially among the young —even among the Protestants. As these symbols and countless bumper stickers testify, Americans are willing to display visible signs of personal belief and preference!

The scapular should be used intelligently as a sign of filial love and dedication, a pledge of Mary-like service, a commitment to live our faith to the fullest, and a petition for the protection and intercession of Our Lady. While one can certainly do this without a visible sign of such intent, many people will still find it a useful non-verbal communication for anyone who might chance to see it.

Such use of the scapular is not as a good luck charm, but as a deeply religious thing. For the use of the scapular Our Lady is said to have promised the user—according to a vision to St. Simon Stock (d. 1265)—many blessings, especially at the hour of death. The Church has always held that it is natural for the Blessed Virgin to extend her maternal care *in a special way* to those who are especially devoted to her.

In practice, one should pick a scapular which harmonizes with his or her tastes. While the cloth scapular is prefered by the Church, it permits the use of a blessed "Scapular Medal"—with an image of the Sacred Heart on one side and that of Our Lady of Mount Carmel with scapulars on the reverse side. The so-called Combination Medal incorporates the Scapular Medal with the Miraculous Medal, that of St. Joseph, St. Christopher, and, often, the Holy Spirit. Because of the large variety of shapes and the bringing together of several devotional medals in one, this medal has a great appeal.

If you should choose to wear the cloth scapular, you should change it before it becomes grimy and, therefore, a displeasing symbol. (After one is properly enrolled, the new, clean scapulars need not be blessed again. A new medal must be blessed.) A special day for renewal of one's dedication to Christ through Mary can be the Memorial to Our Lady of Mount Carmel on July 16.

Fourth, updating prayers of consecration. Since Baptism involves the complete giving of self to God through Christ, the use of a prayer or act of consecration only makes more conscious what happened at Baptism. The classic form of renewal of consecration is the renewal of the baptismal vows. In the last three centuries, many acts of dedication appeared and they all imply a renewal of self-giving to God through Christ or through a saint because of his or her relationship to God. Consecration. should be renewed by inclusion of the baptismal vows and mental renewal at the Offertory of the Mass.

Besides the *ordinary consecration,* which involves

only commitment to what one is already obliged to be as a good Christian, some people like to make an act of *total consecration*. This would involve the intention of making an all-embracing concentration of his or her spiritual life around the Blessed Virgin: to imitate her life which was totally dedicated to Christ. Odilo of Cluny (d. 1049) developed such an idea and it was perfected by St. Grignon de Montfort (d. 1716).

The language of such prayers sometimes speaks of becoming a servant or slave of Mary. One can ask for more suitable updated words but such loving dedication is part of the pluralism of love available for the free choice of the believer. (Several forms of consecration will be found in the Prayer Section at the end of this chapter.)

Fifth updating other Marian devotions. A sure sign of pluralism within the unity of the same faith, the same Eucharistic Sacrifice and Sacraments, and same divine authority, that of Christ who rules his body mystical through the pope and bishops in communion with him is the variety of ways of approaching devotion to Mary and the Saints. The Church asks only that these devotions be doctrinally correct, free of excesses, in good taste, and lead us to Jesus, the sole Mediator with the Father.

Old devotions need not be discarded but merely renewed in the light of the principles in Chapter Two. This often requires only the addition of a liturgical prayer with them (as appears in samples at the end of this chapter) or the addition of phrases or sentences to reflect that doctrinal data obtained from the Church's Magisterium.

138

MARIAN PRAYERS

I. SEASONAL MARIAN PRAYERS:

1. ADVENT SEASON:

Father,
in your plan for our salvation
your Word became man,
announced by an angel and born of the Virgin
Mary.
May we who believe that she is the Mother
of God
receive the help of her prayers.
We ask this through Christ our Lord.

(Sacramentary, Common of the Blessed Virgin Mary.)

2. CHRISTMAS SEASON:

Father,
you gave the human race eternal salvation

through the motherhood of the Virgin Mary.
May we experience the help of her prayers in
our lives,
for through her we receive the very source of
life,
your Son, our Lord Jesus Christ,
who lives and reigns with you and the Holy
Spirit,
one God, for ever and ever.

(Sacramentary, Common of the Blessed Virgin Mary.)

3. *EASTER SEASON:*

God our Father,
you give joy to the world
by the resurrection of your Son,
*   our Lord Jesus Christ.*
Through the prayers of his mother,
*   the Virgin Mary,*
bring us to the happiness of
*   eternal life.*
We ask this through Christ our Lord.

(Sacramentary, **Common** of the **Blessed Virgin**,   6.)

4. *PENTECOST SEASON:*

God our Father,
you gave the Holy Spirit to your
*   apostles*
as they joined in prayer with Mary,
*   the mother of Jesus.*
By the help of her prayers

140

> *keep us faithful in your service*
> *and let our words and actions be*
> * so inspired*
> *as to bring glory to your name.*
> *Grant this through Christ our Lord.*

(Sacramentary, Common of the Blessed Virgin, 6.)

5. *FOR ANY TIME:*

> *Lord God,*
> *give to your people the joy*
> *of continual health in mind and body.*
> *With the prayers of the Virgin Mary*
> * to help us,*
> *guide us through the sorrows of this*
> * life.*
> *Grant this through Christ our Lord.*

(Sacramentary, Common of the Blessed Virgin, 1.)

II. *GENERAL PRAYERS TO OUR LADY:*

1. *THE HAIL HOLY QUEEN*
(SALVE REGINA):

> *Hail, holy Queen, Mother of mercy; hail*
> *our life, our sweetness and our hope. To*
> *you do we cry, poor banished children of Eve.*
> *To you do we send up our sighs, mourning*
> *and weeping in this valley of tears. Turn*
> *then, most gracious Advocate, your eyes of*

mercy toward us. And after this our exile show unto us the blessed fruit of your womb, Jesus, O clement, O loving, O sweet Virgin Mary.

(Partial indulgence, 51.)

2. THE MEMORARE:

Remember, O most gracious Virgin Mary, that never was it ever known that anyone who fled to your protection, implored your help or sought your intercession was left unaided. Inspired with this confidence, I fly to you, O Virgin of virgins, my Mother; to you do I come, before you I stand, sinful and sorrowful. O Mother of the Word Incarnate, despise not my petitions, but in your mercy hear and answer me. Amen.

(Partial indulgence, 32.)

3. THE ANGELUS:

The Angel of the Lord declared unto Mary,
—And she conceived of the Holy Spirit.

Hail Mary....
—Holy Mary....

Behold the handmaid of the Lord,
—Be it done unto me according to your word.

Hail Mary....
—Holy Mary....

And the Word was made flesh,
—And dwelt among us.

Hail Mary . . . .
—Holy Mary . . . .

Pray for us, O holy Mother of God,
—That we may be made worthy of the promises of Christ.

LET US PRAY (p-a-u-s-e):

Pour forth, we beg you, O Lord, your grace
into our hearts: that we, to whom the Incarnation of Christ your Son was made known
by the message of an Angel, may by his
Passion and Cross be brought to the glory
of his Resurrection. Through the same Christ
our Lord. Amen.

(Partial indulgence,   9.)

EASTER "ANGELUS": **REGINA COELI**

Queen of Heaven, rejoice, Alleluia.
For he whom you merited to bear, alleluia.
Has risen as he said, alleluia.
Pray for us to God, alleluia.

Rejoice and be glad, O Virgin Mary, alleluia.
—Because the Lord is truly risen, alleluia.

LET US PRAY (p-a-u-s-e):

O God, who by the Resurrection of your Son,
our Lord Jesus Christ, granted joy to the
whole world: grant, we beg of you, that
through the intercession of the Virgin Mary,
his Mother, we may lay hold of the joys of
eternal life. Through the same Christ our
Lord. Amen.

(Partial indulgence,   9.)

4. ACT OF CONSECRATION - 1:

O Jesus, living in Mary, come and live in your servants, in the spirit of your holiness, in the fullness of your power, in the perfection of your ways, in the truth of your virtues, in the participation of your mysteries: subdue every hostile power in the virtue of your Spirit for the glory of the Father. Amen.

(St. Grignon de Montfort, 1673-1716.)

5. ACT OF CONSECRATION - 2:

Virgin full of goodness, Mother of Mercy, I recommend to you my body and soul, my thoughts, my actions, my life, and my death. O my Queen! help me, and deliver me from all the snares of the devil; obtain for me the grace of loving my Lord Jesus Christ, your Son, with a true and perfect love, and after him, O Mary, to love you with all my heart and above all things. Amen.

(St. Thomas Aquinas, c. 1225-1274.)

6. ACT OF CONSECRATION - 3 - TRADITIONAL:

O Mary, my Queen, my Mother, I give myself entirely to you and to show my devotion to you, I consecrate my eyes, my ears, my mouth, my heart, my whole being without reserve. Therefore, good Mother, as I am

*your own, keep me, guard me, as your son/
daughter. Amen.*

7. ACT OF TOTAL CONSECRATION:

*Most blessed Virgin Mary, I give and con-
secrate myself entirely to you, and through
you to Jesus, our Mediator with the Father.
Because you are now my Queen and Mother,
O Mary, I give and consecrate to you all
my good actions, prayers, desires, and indulgences—past, present, and future—as well as
those which others will offer for me now and
in the future, especially after my death. Use
them as you see fit.*

*While I shall continue to pray for myself,
my family, relatives, friends, those under
my care, or who have asked me to pray for
them, I do so conditionally: do whatever you
know to be best.*

*I also give to you all my merits, graces,
and virtues. Since I cannot give these away
to others, please keep them safe and help
me increase them. Amen.*

8. TO MARY, MOTHER OF THE CHURCH:

*Gracious Lady, you are mother and virgin;
you are the Mother of the body and soul of
our Head and Redeemer; you are also truly
mother of all the members of Christ's Mystical Body. For through your love, you have
cooperated in the begetting of the faithful in*

145

the Church. Unique among women, you are mother and virgin: mother of Christ and Virgin of Christ. You are the beauty and charm of earth, O Virgin. You are forever the image of the holy Church. Through a woman came death; through a woman came life, yes, through you, O Mother of God.

(St. Augustine, 354-430.)

9. CONTEMPORARY MARIAN PRAYER:

God our Father, by the message of an angel, you requested that the humble Virgin of Nazareth place herself at the service of your Providence, so that our redemption could take place through her Son. Because of your choice, you endowed Mary with sublime gifts befitting her future role as Mother of God by the workings of the Spirit and the foreseen merits of Christ. With a heart unimpeded by sin, the Virgin-Mother devoted herself to the person and work of your Son. So perfectly did she receive and practice your word revealed by Christ Jesus, that he extolled her as blessed.

Under inspiration, Father all-holy, the Church recognizes Blessed Mary as spiritual Mother, Mother of the Church, and model of the perfect Christian. Not only did she bring forth and raise the Savior of all, but she lovingly assisted in the offering of this beloved Victim on the Cross of Calvary. Even now, by your will, she continues this saving task through her powerful intercession with

146

you in heaven. Inspired by Scripture, we shall contemplate her many virtues; we thank you for all the favors which you shower on your pilgrim people as we make our way to our Father's home.

Ever inspired by her faith, obedience, hope, and burning charity, may we live in peace and harmony, until we praise you, loving Father, with your Son and our Brother, together with the Holy Spirit, for ever and ever. Amen.

(After Chapter VIII, in the *Dogmatic Constitution on the Church*.)

10. *FOR THE INTERCESSION OF THE IMMACULATE ONE:*

O Virgin, most pure, wholly unspotted, O Mary, Mother of God, Queen of the universe, you are above all the saints, the hope of the elect and the joy of all the blessed. It is you who have reconciled us with God; you are the only refuge of sinners and the safe harbor of those who are shipwrecked; you are the consolation of the world, the ransom of captives, the health of the weak, the joy of the afflicted, and the salvation of all. We have recourse to you, and we beseech you to have pity on us. Amen.

(St. Ephrem the Syrian, died c. 373.)

III. SPECIAL MARIAN DEVOTIONS

1. OUR LADY OF MOUNT CARMEL:

O God,
the order of Carmel was singularly honored
when the title of the most blessed ever-virgin
Mary,
your Mother, was given to it.
Grant that we who commemorate this solemn
feast today
may be shielded by her protection
and attain everlasting happiness:
You who live and reign with God the Father
in the unity of the Holy Spirit,
God, for ever and ever. Amen.

(Roman Missal, Feast of Our Lady of
Mount Carmel.)

*O almighty and eternal God, you willed
that your only-begotten Son should be clothed
in our mortal nature of the Virgin Mary.
I have put on the new man in Baptism, and
wish to add the scapular (medal) of Our Lady
of Mount Carmel as an outward sign of my
dedication to Jesus through his Mother. She
will surely lead me to him. With the prayers
of the Carmelite order to assist me as I wear
their scapular, may I do good, grow in the
love of Jesus and Mary, and attain to the
reward of a blessed eternity with you for
ever and ever. Amen.*

Our Lady of Mount Carmel, pray for me/us.

All through you, with you, and in you, O my God!

(The Raccolta, 29.) *

2. OUR LADY OF SORROWS:

O God,
in your passion the prophesy of Simeon was
fulfilled
that a sword of sorrow should pierce
the soul of your glorious virgin-mother
Mary.
We reverently recall her sufferings and
sorrow.
Mercifully grant us the fruits of your own
sufferings.
You who live and reign .... (above).

(Roman Missal, Feast of the Seven Sorrows of the Blessed Virgin Mary.)

Most holy Virgin and Mother, your life was filled with the joys of motherhood and family life, but also pierced with swords of sorrow and anxiety. Assist me now as I bear the sorrow of............and help me to be attached to God's will as you were. Help me to unite my pain to the Cross of Christ, so that I may someday soon join it to the happi-

---

* A short Trinitarian or Christological prayer should be included with each Marian devotion. (An example of various types will follow each devotion included in this section.)

149

*ness of his Resurrection. As I call out in my
need, help me to be ever mindful of others
in theirs.*

*Our Lady of Sorrows, intercede with your
Son on my/our behalf. Amen.*

*Teach me, O Lord, to do your will, for
you are my God (Ps. 142: 10).*

3. OUR LADY OF PERPETUAL HELP:

*O Lord Jesus Christ,
we venerate the wondrous picture of your
                              Mother Mary.
You gave her to be our mother also,
always ready to help us.
Grant that we who earnestly implore her
                        motherly assistance
may be worthy to enjoy the eternal fruit of
                        your redemption.
You who live and reign....(above).*

(Roman Missal, Feast of the Blessed
Virgin of Perpetual Help.)

*O holy Virgin Mary, who to inspire us with
boundless confidence, has been pleased to
take the tender name of Perpetual Help, I
implore you to come to my aid always and
everywhere, in my temptations, after my
falls , in my difficulties, in all the miseries
of my life, and above all, at the hour of my
death. Count me among your most devoted
servants. Take me under your protection and*

it is enough for me. For if you protect me, dear Mother, I fear nothing: not for my sins, because you will obtain pardon of them; nor from the devils, because you are more powerful than all hell put together; nor from Jesus, my Judge, because by one prayer from you, he will be appeased. But one thing I fear, that in the hour of temptation, I may fail to have recourse to you, and thus perish miserably. Obtain for me, therefore, the pardon of my sins, love of Jesus, final perseverance, and the grace to have recourse to you. Amen.

Mother of Perpetual Help, pray for me/us.

All honor, laud and glory be,
O Jesus, Virgin-born to Thee:
All glory, as is ever meet,
To Father and to Paraclete.

(The Raccolta,   90.)

READINGS FOR MARIAN DEVOTIONS

(More readings will be found on page 158)

(More readings will be found on page 158)

Gen. 3:9-15.

Prov. 8: 22-31.

Sir. 24: 3-21.

Is. 7: 10-14.

Rev. 11: 19; 12: 1-6, 10.

Rom. 5: 12, 17-19.

Gal. 4: 4-7.

Mt. 1: 18-24.

Mt. 2: 13-15. 19-23.

Lk. 1: 26-47.

Lk. 1: 39-56.

Lk. 2: 1-19.

Lk. 2: 27-35.

Lk. 2: 41-52.

Lk. 11: 27-28.

Jn. 2: 1-11.

MARIAN PRAYERS INSPIRED BY APPARITIONS

1. CONTEMPORARY COMBINATION PRAYER:

*O compassionate Father, thank you for calling mankind back again and again into your love and grace. Through the prophets, through your only-begotten Son, through your Church, and even in our times through the apparitions of your beloved daughter, the ever-virgin Mother of your Son, you tell us of man's unfaithfulness and your never-failing willingness to accept his return. Through the **mediation** of your Son and with the prayers of the Virgin Mary joined to ours, we ask for the grace to enter into the mystery of your Son's death by our voluntary mortifications and acceptance of the daily crosses, and into his resurrection by our efforts to be loving, virtuous, and faithful to the duties of our state in life. Like Abraham of old, pleading for the cities of Sodom and Gomorrah (Gen. 18:16-34), lead us through the urgings of the Immaculate One to pray for sinners, while at the same time reforming our own lives. We wish, therefore, Kind God, to offer*

*our entire lives in answer to this call to prayer,
right living, reparation, and concern for others.
Assist us to be hearers of the Word of God who
carry it out most diligently. Then, having been
loved by the Hearts of Jesus and Mary in this
life, may we share the joy of the Trinity for all
eternity. We ask this in faith and in the name of
Christ our Lord. Amen.*

2. OUR LADY OF GUADALUPE:

*God of power and mercy,
you blessed the Americas at Tepeyac
with the presence of the Virgin Mary of Guadalupe.
May her prayers help all men and women
to accept each other as brothers and sisters.
Through your justice present in our hearts
may your peace reign in the world.
We ask this through Christ our Lord.*

(Sacramentary, Our Lady of Guadalupe.)

*O holy Virgin Mary, spotless Queen of the
Americas,
continually at prayer with your beloved Son,
who reigns at the side of the Father: teach us to
raise our hearts
in prayer morning, noon, and night. May the
praise and thanks we offer
on earth continue in the company of the Angels
and Saints for ever
and ever. Amen.*

Our Lady of Guadalupe, pray for me/us.

Most Holy Trinity, we adore you and through
Mary implore you.
Give unto all mankind unity in faith
and courage faithfully to confess it. Amen.

(The Raccolta,   30.)

3. OUR LADY OF THE MIRACULOUS MEDAL (IMMACULATE MARY):

O Lord Jesus Christ,
you have willed to glorify with countless miracles
the Virgin Mary, your Mother,
who was sinless from the first moment of her
existence.
May we always implore her patronage
and so attain the eternal joys of heaven.
You who live and reign with God the Father
in the unity of the Holy Spirit,
One God for ever and ever. Amen.

(Roman Missal, Feast of Blessed
Mary of the Miraculous Medal.)

O Lord Jesus Christ, you chose the weak things
of this world for the accomplishment of your
greatest works, so that no flesh may glory in vain
pride. So you wished that the Miraculous Medal
be revealed to St. Catherine Laboure for a better
and widely diffused belief in the Immaculate
Conception of your Mother. Grant, we beg you,
to be filled with like humility so that we may
glorify this mystery by word and work. You who
live and reign with God the Father in the unity
of the Holy Spirit, One God for ever and ever.
Amen.

All honor, laud and glory be,
O Jesus, Virgin-born to Thee:
All glory, as is ever meet,
To Father and to Paraclete.

(The Raccolta,   90.)

4.   OUR LADY OF LOURDES
(IMMACULATE MARY):

O God,
you prepared a fitting dwelling place for your Son
by preserving the Blessed Virgin immaculate
at the moment of her conception.
Grant health of mind and body to all of us
who celebrate the feast of her apparitions (today).
Through Christ our Lord. Amen.

(Roman Missal, Feast of the Apparitions of
the Immaculate Virgin Mary at Lourdes.)

Oh ever immaculate Virgin, Mother of Mercy,
Health of the Sick, Refuge of Sinners, Comfort-
ress of the Afflicted, you know my wants, my
troubles, my sufferings. Look upon me with
mercy. When you appeared in the grotto of
Lourdes you made it a privileged sanctuary where
you disperse your favors, and where many suffer-
ers have obtained the cure of their infirmities,
both spiritual and corporal. I come, therefore,
with unbounded confidence to implore your
maternal intercession. My loving Mother, obtain
my request. I will try to imitate your virtues so
that I may one day share your company and bless
you in eternity. Amen.

(Traditional.)

Our Lady of Lourdes, pray for me/us.

*Teach me, O Lord, to do your will, for you are
my God* (Ps. 143:10).

5. OUR LADY OF FATIMA (OF THE ROSARY):

Lord,
fill our hearts with your love,
and as you revealed to us by an angel
the coming of your Son as man,
so lead us through his suffering and death
to the glory of his resurrection,
who lives and reigns with you and the Holy Spirit,
one God, for ever and ever.

(Sacramentary, Our Lady of the Rosary.)

AN ACT OF CONSECRATION

(After Pope Pius XII, 1939-1958.)

Queen of the most holy rosary, Help of Christians, and Refuge of Sinners: to you do we consecrate ourselves, as well as the whole Church and the whole world. Obtain for us from God, O Queen of Mercy, a Christ-like reconciliation of nations, as well as those graces which can convert the souls of men. O Queen of Peace, pray for us, and grant peace to the world—a peace built on truth, justice, and the charity of God. Check the ever-increasing torrent of immorality. Arouse in the faithful a love of purity, a practical Christian life, and an apostolic zeal. May the multitude of those who serve God   increase   in merits   and number. Hasten the day when the kingdom of God will be victorious, O Immaculate Heart of Mary, and all nations will be at peace with God and one another. Amen.

O my God, I believe, I adore, I hope, and I love you.
I ask pardon of you for those who do not believe, do not adore, do not hope, and do not love you.

(Prayer made known at Fatima.)

PRAYER OF POPE JOHN XXIII (1958-1963):

Our Lady of Fatima, by virtue of your Immaculate Heart,
obtain for us from Blessed Jesus, the Source of all Graces,
justice, charity, and peace. Amen.
Immaculate Heart of Mary, pray for me/us.

AN ACT OF REPARATION AND CONSECRATION:

O tender Mother of the God-man and of the Church, Lady of the Rosary, and Queen of Peace, it pains us, because we love you, to hear of the insults and doubts cast against your Immaculate Conception, your perpetual virginity, your spiritual and divine Motherhood; to learn that little ones are deprived of a complete knowledge of the Church's teaching about their Mother; or that your images and pictures are not honored. For these offenses we wish to offer reparation to your Immaculate Heart, especially in the form of Commu-

157

nions of reparation on the First Saturdays of the month as you requested at Fatima.

To show our own filial love, we consecrate ourselves to your Immaculate Heart. We intend to live the Christian life to the fullest, and to heed the message you made known in Portugal. We will pray the rosary for sinners and for world peace; we will sacrifice in a spirit of reparation; we will wear your scapular (medal) as a visible sign of our consecration to you, O Mother of God.

Draw all men to your Son, who lives and reigns with the Father and the Holy Spirit, one God, for ever and ever. Amen.

To the King of ages, immortal and invisible, the only God, be honor and glory for ever and ever. Amen.

PRAYER TO BE SAID AT THE END OF EACH DECADE OF THE ROSARY:

O my Jesus, forgive us our sins,
save us from the fires of hell,
lead all souls to heaven,
especially those most in need of your mercy.

MORE READING FOR MARIAN DEVOTIONS

1 Kgs. 8:22-23, 27-30.	Heb. 2:14-18.
2 Crs. 5:6-10. 13-6:2.	Heb. 10:1-10.
Is. 9:1-6.	Rom. 8:28-30.
Jdt. 13:23-26.	Eph. 1:3-12.
Mic. 5:1-4.	Rev. 21:9-14.

7

THE
ROSARY

The great Pope John XXIII asked the Catholic peoples of the world to pray the rosary for the success of the II Vatican Council soon after he announced that he was going to call that Council into being. It seems strange that the very prayer used to ask God's blessing on the Council should be called into question by some in the name of the "renewal" urged by the same Council.

For Pope John, there never was a question of its need and value. The Pope wrote in his spiritual diary, "My day must be one long prayer; prayer is the breath of life. I propose to recite all fifteen decades of the rosary every day, if possible, in the chapel before the Blessed Sacrament." And he did that, as his associates remember! Immediately after celebrating Mass, he said the Joyful Mysteries; after his brief lunch and nap, he said the Sorrowful Mysteries; and, with his house staff, he recited the Glorious Mysteries at 7:30 in the evening.

"The rosary," he wrote, "as an exercise of Christian piety among the faithful of the latin rite, who form a large part of the Catholic family, takes its place for ecclesiastics after Holy Mass and the Breviary, and for the lay folk after their participation in the sacraments. It is a devout form of union with God, and always has a most uplifting effect on the soul." Why, then, does the Holy Father speak so affectionately about this form of prayer as beneficial for spiritual growth?

WHAT IS THE ROSARY ?

The rosary or Chaplet is a prayer form which combines vocal prayer with meditation on the life and work of Christ and his loving Mother. Its basic unit is the "decade", which is made up of one "Our Father", ten "Hail Marys", and one "Glory Be". (The word "decade" eventually comes from the Greek word for ten.) The complete rosary is made up of fifteen decades, but usually only five are recited at a time.

Although it has been traditional in more recent times to say certain prayers *before* the five decades (i.e. the Sign of the Cross, the Apostles' Creed, three Hail Marys—for an increase of faith, hope, and love, and the Glory Be) and *after* the five decades (i.e. the "Hail, Holy Queen"), these additions are not essential elements of the rosary. (Cfr. Pope Paul's repetition of Pope St. Pius V's authoritative description of the rosary in his *Marian Devotions* of 1974—par. 49, and the official list of indulgenced practices, The *Enchiridion of Indulgences* of 1969, no. 48.) If at all possible, though, these extra prayers should be said.

HISTORY OF THE ROSARY

In both the Eastern and Western Rites of the Roman Catholic Church, one finds prayers in concert with Mary, the Mother of God, seeing her Son through her loving eyes. In the Eastern Rites one finds the "Akathistos Hymn", which is a series of odes and prayers of praise in Mary's honor, which frequently uses the word "Hail".

It appears to go back to about the sixth century and reflects the Byzantine theological point of view. In its twenty-four parts one meditatively reflects on the plenitude of the mystery of Christ and the place Mary has in it because she was chosen to be the "Theotokos", the "God-bearer", Mother of Christ God. The Akathistos Hymn is parallel to but not identical with the rosary.

In the Western Rites of the Roman Catholic Church, the origins of the rosary go back deep into the Middle Ages. It was the practice of monasteries to allow all the lay brothers, who could not read, to recite 150 Our Fathers instead of the 150 psalms prayed during the week in the Liturgy of the Hours (Breviary, Divine Office).

In time, the monks taught the laity living around the monastery to pray the 150 Our Fathers in imitation of the Liturgy of the Hours. This sequence of 150 Our Fathers was soon called the "Poor Man's Psalter". One finds various references to it when one reads that the peasants were reciting their "Paters"—the latin word beginning the Our Father (Pater Noster) in European literature.

At first, the ordinary person seems to have counted his Paters on his or her fingers. This was followed with either a small leather pouch with pebbles in it or a cord with knots. The knots in turn gave way to small beads on a string or chain.

In the "Hours of Catherine of Cleves" from about 1440—which is available in a recent facsimile edition—one finds the type with cord and beads as a decoration on one of the pages. Jan van Eyck knew the rosary in this form—as we see in his painting of Giovanni Arnofini and his Bride (1434). Michaelangelo seems to have had this type also in mind when he painted his great fresco of the "Last Judgment" (1534-41) in the Sistine Chapel. He has a saint pulling a soul from Purgatory with the aid of a rosary. And Murillo (d. 1682), to mention another artist, painted a lovely "Madonna of the Rosary" with this early form of rosary. Praying one's "beads" seems clearer in the light of these pictures.

The Our Father was ever so slowly replaced with the Hail Mary. The Hail Mary was originally a much shorter prayer than now. In the beginning of the 6th Century, the words of the angel to Mary (Luke 1:28) were used and no more: "Hail Mary, full of grace, the Lord is with you. Blessed are you among women" Then the words of Elizabeth from Luke's Gospel were included: "And blessed is the fruit of your womb" (1:42). And in 1260, the word "Jesus" was added.

This short Hail Mary was said along with the 150 Our Fathers at first. In time, the Our Fathers were reduced until only a few remained, but 150 Hail Marys were prayed. By the 11th Century, this ancient Hail Mary became a very popular prayer. In the 14th and 15th Centuries, the second half of the Hail Mary was added: "Holy Mary,

Mother of God, pray for us sinners, now and at the hour of our death. Amen."

Since it took a good bit of time to say all these prayers, it was quite natural to divide them into smaller groups. Both Henry Kalkar (d. 1408), a Carthusian monk, and Blessed Alan de la Roche (d. 1475), a Dominican, are given credit for dividing the "Aves" (Hail Marys) into three series of fifty.

Blessed Alan was a great promoter of the rosary, and he gave the Hail Mary a precise form so that it could be prayed publically and universally. He also wrote statements upon which the faithful meditated as they recited the Hail Marys. This same Dominican seems to be the first person to speak of the vision of Our Lady to St. Dominic on the rosary—about two centuries after St. Dominic's time.

THE MEDITATIONS

The large number of similar prayers, then as now, offered the possibility of monotony and distraction, or a point of departure for meditation. It is a problem, yet it yields to openness to grace, perseverance, and technique. At first, people used only one subject of meditation, the Annunciation scene from Luke (1: 26-38). In time, other ideas were drawn from Scripture for meditation—sometimes even as many as 150 sentences were used. Then, to make the Rosary into a communal prayer with meditation, there was a movement to standardize the prayers and the thoughts.

By 1480, the Dominican Order published a booklet entitled *Our Lady's Psalter* with fifteen meditations or mysteries. (Thirteen of them became part of the present fifteen in common use today!) By 1500, the idea of dividing the mysteries into three sets of five decades was adopted. These are the Joyful, the Sorrowful, and the Glorious Mysteries of today, which are listed below under the third suggestion.

The *enduring value of the rosary over the centuries* was precisely in making meditation possible even in the busiest life. Its "quiet rhythm and lingering pace" not only can bring peace to the soul, but—most important—helps the individual to look deeply into the meaning of Christ in his or her life.

Of the many explanations of how this meditation takes place, a Methodist minister, J. Nevill Ward, said it well in his book (later a paperback) entitled *Five for Sorrow, Ten for Joy*. There we read: "As one becomes familiar with the Rosary the prayers gradually recede, to form a kind of 'background' music, and the mystery is before the mind as though one is looking at a religious picture or ikon. The balance frequently changes, and the prayers occupy the foreground of the mind for a time, and this may lead to a form of simple attention to God which is more like contemplation. If one finds one's mind being led into a stillness and concentration of this kind, it is good to let it happen. It is just a fact of Christian history that the saints put their money on contemplation rather than meditation for producing the longing for God".

Pope Paul VI, in his Apostolic Exhortation

Marian Devotion, stresses that the rosary is like a body without a soul, if it is prayed without meditation (n. 47). "The rosary," he wrote, "considers in harmonious succession the principal salvific events accomplished in Christ, from his virgin conception and the mysteries of his childhood to the culminating moments of the Passover —the blessed Passion and the glorious Resurrection—and to the effects of this on the infant Church on the day of Pentecost, and on the Virgin Mary when at the end of her earthly life she was assumed body and soul into her heavenly home.

It has also been observed that the division of the mysteries of the Rosary into three parts not only adheres strictly to the chronological order of the facts, but above all reflects the plan of the original proclamation of the faith and sets forth once more the mystery of Christ in the very way in which it is seen by Saint Paul in the celebrated "hymn" of the Letter to the Philippians—kenosis, death and exaltation (2: 6-11; n. 45). For this reason, the Pope also called the rosary "a Gospel prayer".

This enduring value of meditation can also be sought in many other ways, but for most people it is usually through the rosary or not at all. It is the classical form of vocal prayer leading to meditation for the young to the old, for the sick and the healthy, for almost everyone.

While it is best done in a slow, thoughtful manner, many are drawn to it as they make their way to work, while driving, or going about other activities. While meditation suffers when one is half occupied with something else, one cannot fault them from praying in this way. This is especially true of those who suffer. For many, then, this will be the usual and only way in which they meditate, and it is a very legitimate way too.

THE ROSARY AND THE LITURGY

Some wish to say the rosary during the liturgy, while others so stress the Eucharistic Sacrifice that they see no further usefulness for the rosary. Pope Paul VI teaches what the best tradition of the Church has always been: "Liturgical celebrations and the pious practice of the Rosary must be neither set in opposition to one another nor considered as being identical. The more the expression of prayer preserves its own true nature and individual characteristic, the more fruitful it becomes" (ibidem, n. 48).

While both receive inspiration from the Bible, there is a difference between them. The rosary familiarizes the mind and heart with the meaning of Christ to move oneself to live that meaning in his or her life. The liturgy, on the other hand, is on another plane of reality: Christ becomes present in the People of God, especially in his Word and in the Sacrament, to offer the great hymn of praise and thanks to God, to become mankind's pleasing sacrifice to the Father, and its food on the pilgrimage to heaven.

Christ is present where two or three are gathered in his name, but in quite different ways in the case of the rosary and the Mass. Because one cannot focus at Mass on the salvific action of Christ, while at the same time doing something else which requires the whole mind and heart, Pope Paul states so clearly: "However, it is a mistake to recite the rosary during the celebration of the liturgy, though unfortunately this practice still persists here and there" (ibidem, n. 48). Because of the differing natures of each prayer form, the pope declined to accept the suggestion of some to designate the rosary as an official liturgical prayer of the Mystical Body—the Church united with Christ its Head. He urged the rosary as a prayer of meditation which can serve as a preparation for the liturgy and as a way of making the liturgy more fruitful in one's life.

UPDATING THE ROSARY

Before making any specific suggestions, it might be well to make the point that there are *still* several ways of praying the rosary, even though the Latin Church has preferred the Dominican manner since Pope St. Pius V picked this one out for general promotion and use in 1569. (For example, the Bridgitine Rosary has six decades, each ending with the Creed.)

The Latin Rite has selected the Dominican Rosary for use in church and official gatherings. There is no official intent at this time to do away with time-honored alternate ways of saying the rosary, nor to eliminate new creative ways of praying the rosary alone or in private gathering. Hence, if the present way of praying the rosary serves well, use it; if not, perhaps one should give a new way a chance. So, what can be done to update the rosary?

First, go to the Scriptures, either before saying the rosary or in connection with the praying of the rosary, to read the source of the meditation. If one reads the whole passage through or meditates on it line by line, with the Hail Marys flowing in between, it can only but improve the meditation.

In this connection, one might like to use a little booklet which suggests 150 sentences—one for each "Ave". Three good ones are: *The Scriptural Rosary, Our Lady's Psalter,* and *Ten Series of Meditations on the Mysteries of the Rosary*—this latter also presents ideas from the writings of the saints and popes. (Cfr. below for the scriptural source of the meditations.)

Second, the rosary might have a greater effect in one's prayer life if it were more closely harmonized with the Liturgical Year. Just as the Mass and the Liturgy of the Hours develops Christ's life and ideas in the course of a year (Advent, Christmas, Epiphany, Lent, Passiontide, Holy Week, Easter, Ascension, Pentecost, etc.), so the rosary concentrates on these same mysteries and seasons.

For example, one could say the Joyful Mysteries more frequently during the Advent and Christmas Season, the Sorrowful Mysteries during Lent, and the Glorious Mysteries during the Easter Season. For private use, there is nothing wrong with using all the Easter appearances of Christ, at that time of year, instead of considering the Ascension, the Descent of the Holy Spirit, the Assumption, and the Coronation of the Blessed Virgin. There are more than enough incidents to make up several decades of meditation.

Third, either individually or in communal use, you might like to include mention of the mystery right within the Hail Mary itself. This may sound novel to some, but it has been done for a long time among the Germans, Austrians, and Slavs of many areas.

"As is well known," states Pope Paul in "Marian Devotions", "at one time there was a custom, still preserved in certain places, of adding to the name Jesus in each Hail Mary a reference to the mystery being contemplated. And this was done precisely in order to help contemplation and to make the mind and voice act in unison" (n. 46). The following ideas have been adapted from a prayerbook for Byzantine-Slavonic Rite Catholics. One adds these lines immediately after the word "Jesus" in the middle of the "Ave".

I. *JOYFUL MYSTERIES:*

1) Jesus, Who was heralded by the Angel (or, Jesus, Who was conceived by the Holy Spirit);
2) Jesus, Whom you carried to visit Elizabeth;
3) Jesus, Who was born of you in Bethlehem;
4) Jesus, Whom you presented in the temple;
5) Jesus, Whom you found again in the temple.

171

II. *SORROWFUL MYSTERIES:*

1) Jesus, Who suffered in agony in the garden;

2) Jesus, Who was scourged for us;

3) Jesus, Who was crowned with thorns;

4) Jesus, Who carried the Cross for us;

5) Jesus, Who was crucified for us.

III. *GLORIOUS MYSTERIES:*

1) Jesus, Who rose gloriously for us;

2) Jesus, Who triumphantly ascended into heaven;

3) Jesus, Who sent the Spirit upon the Apostles;

4) Jesus, Who took you into heavenly glory;

5) Jesus, Who crowned you queen of all.

(An authoritative decision was made by the proper Congregation at the Vatican that such additions, or the little prayer requested by Our Lady at Fatima, do not negate any grant of indulgences for the recitation of the rosary.)

Fourth, You might "invent" new mysteries for your meditation. The American Bishops suggest this in their document, "Behold Your Mother": "Besides the precise rosary pattern long known to Catholics, we can freely experiment. New sets of mysteries are possible" (n. 97). While this is again contemplated for private use for the present, it will open up the whole richness of the Bible for our meditations. Since there are seven days of the week, why not develop seven sets of mysteries— and so expose yourself to the entire history of salvation? A tentative outline of such mysteries might be:

I. *GENESIS MYSTERIES:* (Mondays)

1) God is infinitely perfect and happy: Psalm 145: 1-13-21.
2) God creates to show his love and goodness: Psalm 19: 1-5.
3) God created the world and man: Genesis 1: 1-31.
4) God tested man's love, but man failed: Genesis 3: 1-13.
5) God promised a Redeemer: Genesis 3: 14-16.

II. *PREPARATION FOR THE REDEEMER:* (Tuesdays)

1) The Israelites are chosen by God: Genesis 12: 1-3 or Hosea 11: 1-9.
2) God makes a covenant with them at Sinai: Exodus 19: 2-9.
3) The kings and prophets helped in this plan of God: Psalm 132: 11-18.
4) The covenant is broken by sin again and again: Isaiah 5: 1-7; Psalm 106.
5) God remained faithful to the covenant: Psalm 105; Isaiah 49: 8f.

III. *JOYFUL MYSTERIES:* (Wednesdays)

1) The Annunciation: Luke 1: 26-38.

173

2) The Visitation: Luke 1:39-56.

3) The Birth of Christ: Luke 2:1-19.

4) The Presentation in the Temple: Luke 2:22-40.

5) Finding the Youthful Jesus in the Temple: Luke 2:41-51.

IV. *DOCTRINAL MYSTERIES:* (Thursdays)

1) Jesus is the "the way, the truth, and the life": John 14:1-7.

2) Jesus teaches us to love God with our whole being: Luke 10:25-37.

3) Jesus teaches us to love and forgive: Matthew 5, 43-48; 18, 21-35.

4) Jesus teaches great love for the poor and needy: Matthew 12:15-21; Luke 14:12-15.

5) Jesus urges a loving community: John 15:9-17.

V. *SORROWFUL MYSTERIES:* (Fridays)

1) Jesus suffers the agony in the garden: Luke 22:39-46.

2) Jesus is scourged at the pillar: John 19:1-3.

3) Jesus is crowned with thorns: Matthew 27:27-31.

4) Jesus carries the cross to Calvary: Matthew 27:32-35.

5) Jesus, our Savior, dies for our salvation: Matthew 27:36-56; Philippians 2:6-11.

VI. *GLORIOUS MYSTERIES:* (Saturdays)

1) Jesus is raised from the dead: John 20:1-18.
2) Jesus ascends into heavenly glory: Luke 24:50-53.
3) The Spirit is sent upon the Apostles: Acts 2:1-12, 37-38.
4) Mary is assumed into heaven: Judith 13:23-31.
5) Mary is crowned queen of heaven and earth: Revelations 12.

VII. *THE FINAL MYSTERIES:* (Sundays)

1) Jesus is head of all men and creation: Ephesians 1:3-14.
2) Jesus lives and reigns in his Church: Colossians 1:24-29; Matthew 28:16-20.
3) Jesus will be our eternal reward: Colossians 1:15-23.
4) Jesus will judge the living and the dead: Revelations 20:11-14; 21:1f.
5) Jesus gives all things to the Father: Ephesians 2:1-10.

Fifth, you can add to the traditional or experimental rosary a special intention for each decade. Archbishop Sheen, while being national director of the Society for the Propagation of the Faith, suggested praying for the major mission areas of the world. He even devised a rosary with five different colored decades. He suggested green for

Africa, red for the Americas, white for Europe, blue for Australia and Oceania, and yellow for Asia.

Besides one mission area for each decade, one can pray for five very important needs of the Church —perhaps those suggested in the Holy Father's monthly or mission intention (Apostleship of Prayer). Again, one might think of the needs of our brothers who have different religious beliefs than we do. There are any number of possibilities which might motivate a better praying of the rosary.

Finally, you might like to use "Rosary II" *for private use.* Rosary II is another way of praying the rosary, with its own unique plan for encouraging meditation. The inspiration for Rosary II came from Pope Paul VI's encyclical, *The Month of October,* issued on October 7, 1971. In it the Pope suggests that something might be done to "adapt the rosary to present needs".

After much discussion, various groups thought that meditation might be inspired if less vocal prayer was said and more Scripture was used in connection with the rosary. To achieve this, the groups went back to the short ancient Hail Mary, which ended at the word "Jesus". They plan to begin with the reading of a definite Gospel passage. It would be summarized in a single line or phrase, which would be inserted after the name of Jesus in each short "Ave".

The basic grouping of prayers would still be the decade of ten Hail Marys. At the end of the five decades of one Our Father and ten Hail Marys, the Glory Be would be recited once. The value of Rosary II lies in the use of Scripture and the slower recitation of the prayers—using as much time for the shorter "Ave" as other people use for the usual, longer one.

As yet, this style of praying the rosary has not been submitted to the competent Church authority for approval in the Universal Church. It is still pretty much of a European experience for private prayer. Naturally, it can be used for private prayer, but it should not be encouraged for public church use. Rosary II might help some people who need an alternate form of the rosary to use along with the usual Dominican form.

Regardless of the old or new techniques which one may use to "update" or "renew" the rosary, Pope Paul warns: "The rosary is an excellent prayer, but the faithful should feel serenely free in its regard. They should be drawn to its calm recitation by its intrinsic appeal" (*Marian Devotions*, n. 55). Hopefully the appeal of its enduring value is clear from these pages and one "recognizes its suitability for fostering contemplative prayer—prayer of both praise and petition—and recalls its intrinsic effectiveness for promoting Christian life and apostolic commitment" (ibidem, 42).

HOW TO PRAY THE ROSARY

I. THE MECHANICS OF THE ROSARY:

1. *On the Crucifix*—Sign of the Cross (optional).

2. *On the Crucifix*— **Apostles'** Creed (optional).

3. *First large bead*—Our Father (optional).

4. *Next three beads*—Three Hail Marys for an increase of faith, hope, and love of God (optional).

5. *Before the next big bead*—Glory Be (optional).

6. *On the big bead near the medal*—Think of the First Mystery and say the Our Father.

THE MYSTERIES:

A. JOYFUL MYSTERIES:

1) The Annunciation: Read Luke 1: 26-38.

2) The Visitation: Luke 1: 39-56.

3) The Birth of Christ: Luke 2: 1-19.

4) The Presentation: Luke 2: 22-40.

5) The Finding in the Temple: Luke 2: 41-52.

B. *SORROWFUL MYSTERIES:*

1) The Agony in the Garden: Luke 22: 39-46.

2) The Scourging at the Pillar: John 19: 1-3.

3) The Crowning with Thorns: Matthew 27: 27-31.

4) The Carrying of the Cross: Matthew 27: 32-35.

5) The Crucifixion: Matthew 27: 35-56.

C. *GLORIOUS MYSTERIES:*

1) The Resurrection: Mark 16: 1-14.

2) The Ascension: Luke 24: 50-53.

3) The Descent of the Holy Spirit: Acts 2: 1-12.

4) The Assumption of Mary into heaven: Judith 13: 23-31.

5) The Coronation: Revelations 12.

7. *Next ten beads* —Ten Hail Marys, while meditating on the Mystery.

8. *After 10th bead* —Glory Be.

9. *After Glory Be* —The Fatima Prayer (O my Jesus) (Optional).

10. *Next 4 sets of* —Repeat Steps 6-9, for an

179

large and small beads	additional four decades, but use a different part of the mystery for each.
11. *On the medal*	—The "Hail, Holy Queen" Prayer (optional), with additional ending prayer (optional).
12. *On Crucifix*	—Kiss crucifix and make the Sign of the Cross.

II. PRAYERS NEEDED TO SAY THE ROSARY:

THE SIGN OF THE CROSS:

In the name of the Father, and of the Son, and of the Holy Spirit. Amen.

(Partial indulgence, 55.)

THE APOSTLES' CREED:

I believe in God the Father Almighty, Creator of heaven and earth; and in Jesus Christ, his only Son Our Lord; who was conceived by the Holy Spirit, born of the Virgin Mary, suffered under Pontius Pilate, was crucified, died and was buried. He descended into hell; the third day he arose again from the dead; he ascended into heaven, sits at the right hand of God, the Father Almighty; from thence he shall come to judge the living and the dead. I believe in the Holy Spirit, the Holy Catholic Church, the communion of saints, the forgiveness of sins, the resur-

rection of the body, and life everlasting.
AMEN.

(Partial indulgence, 16.)

THE OUR FATHER:

Our Father, who art in heaven, hallowed
be thy name. Thy kingdom come, Thy will
be done on earth as it is in heaven.

Give us this day our daily bread, and forgive us our trespasses as we forgive those
who trespass against us; and lead us not into
temptation, but deliver us from evil. AMEN.

THE HAIL MARY:

Hail Mary, full of grace! The Lord is with
you, blessed are you among women, and
blessed is the fruit of your womb, Jesus.

Holy Mary, Mother of God, pray for us
sinners, now and at the hour of our death.
AMEN.

THE GLORY BE:

Glory be to the Father, and to the Son, and
to the Holy Spirit. As it was in the beginning, is now, and ever shall be, world without
end. AMEN.

(OPTIONAL FATIMA PRAYER:

O my Jesus, forgive us our sins, save us
from the fires of hell, lead all souls to heaven,
especially those most in need of your mercy.)

THE HAIL, HOLY QUEEN:

Hail, Holy Queen, Mother of mercy,
our life, our sweetness and our hope.
To you do we cry, poor banished children
of Eve,
to you do we send up our sighs,
mourning and weeping in this vale of tears.
Turn, then, most gracious advocate,
your eyes of mercy toward us;
and after this exile, show us the blessed
fruit of your womb, Jesus.
O Clement, O loving, O sweet Virgin Mary.

(Partial indulgence, 51.)

(Note: not everyone memorizes this ending or uses it.)

*Pray for us, O holy Mother of God,
that we may be worthy of the promises of Christ.*

LET US PRAY

O God, whose only-begotten Son, by his life, death, and resurrection, has purchased for us the rewards of eternal salvation; grant, we beseech you, that meditating upon these mysteries in the most holy Rosary of the Blessed Virgin Mary, we may imitate what they contain, and obtain what they promise. Through the same Christ our Lord. AMEN.

(A partial indulgence can be gained whenever the Sign of the Cross (55) and the Apostles' Creed (16), and the Hail, Holy Queen—minus the longer ending (51) are used by themselves.)

(A plenary indulgence can be gained whenever the rosary is said in church, in a family group, or as part of another religious grouping. (Vocal recitation—even if only quietly to oneself—is required for the indulgence.) A partial indulgence is gained in all other circumstances but the above. The same indulgences can be gained for praying the "Acthistos" Hymn, the Office "Paraclisis", or other prayers in honor of Our Lady selected by the Patriarchs.)

ACATHIST HYMN: TWENTY-THIRD CHANT:

By singing praise to your maternity, we all exalt you as the spiritual temple, O Mother of God! For the One who dwelt within your womb, the Lord who holds all things in his hands, sanctified you, glorified you and taught all men to sing to you:

Hail, O Tabernacle of God the Word;
hail, Holy One, more holy than the saints!
Hail, O Ark that the Spirit has gilded;
hail, inexhaustible Treasure of life!
Hail, precious Crown of rightful authorities;
hail, sacred Glory of reverent priests!
Hail, unshakable Tower of the Church;
hail, unbreakable Wall of the Kingdom!
Hail, O you through whom the trophies are raised!
hail, O you through whom the enemies are routed!
Hail, O Healing of my body;
hail, O Salvation of my soul!

183

Hail, O bride and Maiden ever-pure!

Response: *Hail, O Bride and Maiden ever-pure!*

(Common to several Oriental Rites.)

READINGS FOR ROSARY DEVOTIONS

(Cfr. Fourth suggestion for Updating above.)

WITH THE SPREAD OF THIS DEVOTION
(THE ROSARY),
THE MEDITATIONS OF THE FAITHFUL
HAVE BECOME MORE ARDENT
AND THEIR PRAYERS MORE FERVENT,
AND THEY QUICKLY BECOME DIFFERENT
MEN.

(Pope St. Pius V, 1504-1572.)

8

DEVOTIONS
TO AND WITH
THE SAINTS

In 1959, a Catholic weekly newspaper printed in bold type the tongue-in-cheek advertisement: "Mr. Christopher medals still available!" It was a response to the mistaken conclusion that some Saints were demoted from being Saints through the Apostolic Letter, *Mysterium Paschalis*, which approved the revised Roman Calendar. To better accentuate the feasts of Our Lord, all those Saints which did not have world-wide meaning were eliminated from the universal calendar. Like Saint Christopher, the 3rd century martyr about whom we know very few facts, they were not denied the veneration of the faithful, but offered for inclusion in those local calendars where the Saints were known and loved.

CATHOLIC DOCTRINE
ABOUT THE SAINTS

The Church definitely honors certain individuals as Saints who practiced heroic virtue, which has survived a lengthy process of scrutiny *and* confirmation through miracles obtained from God through their intercession. This belief and practice lies within those great mysteries of the absolutely gratuitous nature of justification by Christ through faith and God's respect for the free will which he has given to human beings.

God must initiate, continue, and bring to fruit any human action which is to have a supernatural character, but he still requires free cooperation with his divine gifts. Christ said: "No one comes to me unless the Father who sent me draws him" (Jn. 6: 44). St. Paul said of this absolute need of Christ: "I repeat, it is owing to his favor that salvation is yours through faith. It is not your own doing, it is God's gift; neither is it a reward for anything that you have accomplished, so let no one pride himself on it" (Eph. 2: 8-9).

While no one can save himself of himself through good works, good works are not only a consequence of accepting salvation from Christ, but also a responsibility which God asks of us with his ample help. "What good is it to profess faith without practicing it? ... Be assured, then, that faith without good works is as dead as the body without breath" (James 2: 14-28).

It could hardly be otherwise, since Christ said that he would award salvation to those who believe and condemnation to those who refuse to believe, and eternal life to those who served him in their neighbor and punishment to those who refused to serve him in their neighbor (Matt. 25: 31-46).

Within these two great mysteries of grace and freedom, we find the Saints. They cooperated whole-heartedly with grace, while lesser human beings offered less or compromised. Long before the Church reminds us that "the fervent prayers of a holy man is powerful indeed" (James 5: 15), she sees God acting *in* and *through* these persons.

Yes, God acts through them as Christ uses them to apply the fruits of redemption in another time and place. They are useful to Christ and to the People of God, and this usefulness does not end with death. Because the saint loves more, not less, in the greater clarity of love which results from the possession of God in heaven, the saint would be more willing, not less able, to serve the Pilgrim Church.

The Church proposes that the Saints are useful to us on several grounds. First, they are proofs of God's great love for us and his willingness to give us his gifts of grace—if we are willing to cooperate with him. Second, they are models of Christ-like lives which we can imitate or, at least, admire. Finally, they are friends of God who can add their more powerful prayers to ours as we pray to the Father through Christ. Since God is glorified in his Saints (2 Tim. 1: 10), he is even more glorified when more individuals (Christ, the Saints, ourselves) adore him, petition for needs, offer him contrition, and thank him for his gifts.

The beautiful gospel story of the Centurion asking for the cure of his servant is a way of visualizing the intercession of the Saints. First he petitions through friendly Jewish officials then through his friends. The soldier knew that Jesus would, no doubt, listen to him, but he was a humble man. He knew that Christ would see him as he really was—much as God sees us for the sinners we are when we pray to him. So, the Centurion asked others to petition for his favor *in his behalf* and *with* him.

This short story from Luke's account (7: 1-10) shows us how to regard the Saints. They do not take our place. No, they lovingly add their prayers to ours as we pray through our beloved Mediator, Christ Jesus, to the heavenly Father. The prayers of the Saints intensify, as it were, our prayers by being added to our own. Because the Saints are God's proven friends, that prayer will receive a merciful hearing from the God who answers all prayers for our long-ranged good.

THE TEACHING OF THE COUNCIL

The II Vatican Council re-echoed the teaching of other great Councils before it on the Saints. Orthodox doctrine has always maintained that devotion to the Blessed Virgin and the Saints must always be subordinated to the fact of the mediatorship of Christ. Since the Incarnation, Redemption, and Glorification of Christ, all things have been handed over to his lordship. He gave himself as ransom for all (1 Tim. 2: 5-6) and, now, he brings all blessings to us.

Within the lordship of Christ, the duty to love and care for each other has not disappeared. Hence, even within the total mediation of Christ, there is room for the intercession of the Saints. In Chapter Seven of the *Dogmatic Constitution on the Church,* one finds the teaching of the contemporary Church on the Saints. (That chapter bears the name of "The Eschatological Nature of the Pilgrim Church and Its Union with the Church in Heaven".)

The Council taught that the Saints are to be held in the traditional honor which the Church has given to them in the past. Their images and authentic relics are to be honored. Their feast days are to be judged either of universal or local interest to the Church and assigned to either universal or local calendar. Veneration of the Saints is to be rendered *in and with Christ, and through him to the Father.*

Individual Christians should render honor to the Saints through the liturgy as the Church gathers at prayer. Deficient understanding of correct doctrine or poor practice in regard to the Saints is to be improved, but veneration of the Saints is every bit as much a part of the life of the Church as it ever was. Within the mediation and lordship of Christ, the Saints, the Angels, and ourselves form one mighty chorus of loving praise and thanksgiving to the Father of all. Both liturgical and devotional prayer form part of this mighty chorus of love.

UPDATING VENERATION
OF THE SAINTS

The great liturgist, Rev. Josef Jungmann, S.J., suggests that we follow the lead of the Church herself in our veneration of the saints by observing what she does.

First, we see that the Church has not eliminated the honoring of the Saints from her life, but rather distinguished between universal and particular appeal. Not every saint has something to say to modern times apart from the perpetual message of loving imitation of Christ. Since this is so, the Church has picked those Saints who do have a particular trait or message for our times for inclusion in her official universal calendar of feasts. As for the rest, she offers them for local and personal use.

In the same way, we should try to understand why particular Saints have been singled out, find their characteristic way of loving God, serving neighbor and imitating Christ, and follow their lead. As a *basic minimum,* we should offer that general veneration offered by the Church herself.

In each and every liturgy, she offers honor to the Blessed Virgin and the Saints and begs their intercession in the Eucharistic Prayer. Besides this, she offers the Opening Prayer, the Prayer-over-the-Gifts, and the Prayer-after-Communion in honor of the individual saint who is remembered once a year on his or her feast day. This is fitting, since each saint is a proof of God's goodness and the

successful completion of human effort in cooperation with his grace.

Second, the Church now offers priests, religious
and laity the example of the Liturgy of the Hours
as a means of learning about Saints. In the Hour
of Reading, there is a brief biography of the saint
of the day, based on the best scholarship available.
This is usually followed by a quotation from the
saint's writings to act as spiritual reading and inspiration.

When such writings are not available, a writing
about the saint is used, in which the author explains how the saint became a saint or which virtue
of the saint is beneficial for our times. The stress
of another generation on the miraculous has been
replaced with a desire to see the saint as a human
being: to learn how he or she imitated Christ so
well in his love of God and neighbor so that he
became a saint.

In your own spiritual life, you could make more
use of these liturgical readings of the Church.
While not neglecting modern authors, you can see
a great advantage in considering the words of those
who have actually "made it" to heaven.

Third, the Litany of the Saints could be used
with some regularity. One should observe its general pattern and observe it in venerating the saints.

This prayer begins with adoration of the Father,
Son and Holy Spirit. It moves on to veneration of
the Blessed Virgin, St. Joseph, and the people
closest to Christ in his human life. Saints from all
periods of Church history and from all walks of

life are honored and asked for assistance. Petitions follow for all the needs of suffering humanity. Finally, the litany closes with a gathering of all our thoughts and desires through Christ with the Holy Spirit to God the Father.

In so honoring the Saints, the Church never loses sight nor deflects from the main melody of love and adoration which is offered "through Christ, with Christ, and in Christ" to the glory of the Trinity. Unless we misdirect our veneration of the Saint into a "give me, give me, give me" practice, we can learn the *correct and liturgical* pattern for honoring the Saints from the Litany of the Saints.

Again, in public and private devotions and novenas, we should follow the general outlines of the Liturgy of the Word at Mass. Without slavish imitation, one sees the elements: a greeting, penitential rite, readings, responses, a homily or explanation, and prayers of the faithful.

Special novena prayers to the saint could be inserted as a response to a reading, follow the explanation or serve as a conclusion to the prayers of the faithful. The connection with the Liturgical Year can be established by using a reading, response or Opening Prayer from the Mass of the previous Sunday. A hymn can be sung or recited which also gives the seasonal flavoring.

In matters of readings, one is not bound to just scriptural readings in services outside of Mass. One could use the readings from the Liturgy of the Hours or a select quotation from the writings or biography of the saint. One could also learn from the recent *Directory for Masses with Children* (1973) that visual elements can be used effectively, if done with *prudence*. (If the Church allows it at such Masses, then she certainly would offer more elasticity in non-liturgical and para-liturgical services.) Among those visual elements would be a greater use of liturgical symbols, candles, lights, pictures, banners, even playlets, and so on. (Cfr. *Directory for Masses with Children*, n. 35-36.)

To eliminate the charge that novenas and devotions are too self-centered, one could make better use of the general intercessions—and see that they really are *general*. Each day of the novena could be dedicated to the needs of some particular group. One novena series might consider the needs of each continent of the earth. Another might consider the problems of various occupational groups, states in life, and so on. Another might just look at how bad the world is and prayerfully do something about it.

Finally, the priest might ask for "input" from the congregation by passing out cards for this purpose beforehand. Even the format of these prayers should be changed from time to time—sometimes responding to the priest's prayer, sometimes alternating with him, sometimes praying the whole prayer together.

Finally, one should re-evaluate old prayers in the light of the liturgy and continually use the really fine Opening Prayers from the Common for the Saints. They summarize the Church's whole teaching and practice in the matter of honoring the Saints. By using them regularly, one will keep the correct dogmatic and liturgical balance in devotional prayers to the Saints.

PRAYERS TO AND WITH THE SAINTS

I. LITANY OF THE SAINTS

In this updated, official Litany, in those sections marked "A" or "B", only one or the other has to be used. For a shorter, official Litany, use only those phrases marked*. For group use, a leader or first group can recite the first half of each prayer, and the rest answer with the response. (Patron and local saints may be added where appropriate.)

I. PETITIONS TO GOD

A.

*Lord, have mercy.   *Lord, have mercy.
*Christ, have mercy.   *Christ, have mercy.
*Lord, have mercy.   *Lord, have mercy.

B.

God our Father in heaven,   have mercy on us.

God the Son, our redeemer,   have mercy on us.
God the Holy Spirit,   "
Holy Trinity, one God,   "

II. PETITIONS TO THE SAINTS

*Holy Mary,   pray for us.
*Mother of God,   "
 Most honored of all virgins,   "
*Michael, Gabriel and Raphael,   "
*Angels of God,   "

Prophets and Fathers of our Faith

 Abraham, Moses and Elijah,   pray for us.
*St. John the Baptist,   "
*Saint Joseph,   "
 Holy Patriarchs and prophets,   "

Apostles and Followers of Christ

*Saint Peter and Saint Paul,   pray for us.
*Saint Andrew,   "
*Saint John and Saint James,   "
 Saint Thomas,   "
 Saint Matthew,   "
 All holy apostles,   "
 Saint Luke,   "
 Saint Mark,   "
 Saint Barnabas,   "
*Saint Mary Magdalen,   "
 All disciples of the Lord,   "

Martyrs

*Saint Stephen,   pray for us.
*Saint Ignatius,   "

Saint Polycarp,	pray for us.
Saint Justin,	"
*Saint Lawrence,	"
Saint Cyprian,	"
Saint Boniface,	"
Saint Stanislaus,	"
Saint Thomas Becket,	"
Saint John Fisher and Saint Thomas More,	"
Saint Paul Miki,	"
Saint Isaac Jogues and Saint John de Brebeuf,	"
Saint Peter Chanel,	"
Saint Charles Lwanga,	"
*Saint Perpetua and Saint Felicity,	"
*Saint Agnes,	"
Saint Maria Goretti,	"
All holy martyrs for Christ,	"

Bishops and Doctors

Saint Leo and Saint Gregory,	pray for us.
Saint Ambrose,	"
Saint Jerome,	"
*Saint Augustine,	"
*Saint Athanasius,	"
*Saint Basil and Saint Gregory,	"
Saint John Chrysostom,	"
*Saint Martin,	"
Saint Patrick,	"
Saint Cyril and Saint Methodius,	"
Saint Charles Borromeo,	"
Saint Francis de Sales,	"
Saint Pius,	"

Priests and Religious

Saint Anthony,	*pray for us.*
*Saint Benedict,	"
Saint Bernard,	"
*Saint Francis and Saint Dominic,	"
Saint Thomas Aquinas,	"
Saint Ignatius Loyola,	"
*Saint Francis Xavier,	"
Saint Vincent de Paul,	"
*Saint John Vianney,	"
Saint John Bosco,	"
Saint Catherine,	"
Saint Theresa,	"
Saint Rose,	"

Laity

Saint Louis,	*pray for us.*
Saint Monica,	"
Saint Elizabeth,	"
*All holy men and women,	"

III. PETITIONS TO CHRIST

A.

*Lord, be merciful,	Lord, save your people.
*From all evil,	"
*From every sin,	"
From the snares of the devil,	"
From anger and hatred,	"
*From every evil intention,	"
*From everlasting death,	"
*By your coming as man,	"
By your birth,	"
By your baptism and fasting,	"

199

By your sufferings and
  cross,   Lord, save your people.
                                          „
*By your death and burial,   „
*By your rising to new life,   „
 By your return in glory to the Father, „
*By your gift of the Holy Spirit,   „
 By your coming again in glory,   „

B.

Christ, Son of the living God, have mercy on us.
You came into this world,   „
You suffered for us on the cross,   „
You died to save us,   „
You lay in the tomb,   „
You rose from the dead,   „
You returned in glory to the Father,   „
You sent the Holy Spirit upon
  your Apostles,   „
You are seated at the right hand of
  the Father,   „
You will come again to judge
  the living and the dead,   „

IV. PETITIONS FOR VARIOUS NEEDS
       (Others may be added.)

A.

*Lord, be merciful to us,   Lord, hear our prayer.
 Give us true repentance,   „
 Strengthen us in your service,   „
 Reward with eternal life all who do
   good to us,   „

200

Bless the fruits of the earth and of
  man's labor,   "

B.

Lord, show us your
  kindness,   Lord, hear our prayer.
Raise our thoughts and desires to you, "
Save us from final damnation,   "
Save our friends and all who have
  helped us,   "
Grant eternal rest to all who have
  died in the faith,   "
Spare us from disease, hunger,
  and war,   "
Bring all peoples together in trust
  and peace,   "

C—always used

*Guide and protect your
  holy Church,   Lord, hear our prayer.
*Keep the pope and all the
  clergy in faithful service
  to your Church,   "
*Bring all Christians together in unity, "
*Lead all men to the light of the Gospel, "

V. CONCLUDING PRAYERS

A.

*Christ, hear us.
*Christ, hear us.
*Lord Jesus, hear us.
*Lord Jesus, hear us.

B.

Lamb of God, you take away the sins of the world, have mercy on us.

Lamb of God, you take away the sins of the world, have mercy on us.

Lamb of God, you take away the sins of the world, have mercy on us.

PRAYERS

God of love, our strength and protection,
hear the prayers of your Church.
Grant that when we come to you in faith
our prayers may be answered
through Christ our Lord.

or

Lord God, you know our weakness,
In your mercy
grant that the example of your Saints
may bring us back to love and serve you
through Christ our Lord.

(Partial Indulgence, 29.)

II. OTHER PRAYERS IN HONOR OF THE SAINTS AND ANGELS:

1. TRADITIONAL PRAYER TO OUR LADY:

We fly to your protection, O holy Mother of God.

Despise not our petitions in our necessities,
but deliver us always from all dangers,
O glorious and blessed Virgin. Amen.

(Partial Indulgence, 57.)

2. *PRAYER TO ST. JOSEPH:*

God our Father,
creator and ruler of the universe,
in every age you call man
to develop and use his gifts for the good of
others.
With St. Joseph as our example and guide,
help us to do the work you have asked
and come to the rewards you have promised.
We ask this through Christ our Lord.

(Sacramentary, May 1, Joseph the Worker.)

3. *PRAYER TO ONE'S PATRON SAINT:*

O heavenly Patron, N.,
whose memory I honor,
pray ever to God for/with me.
strengthen me in my faith,
establish me in virtue;
guard me in the conflict;
that I may resist temptation
and attain to everlasting glory. Amen.

4. *LITURGICAL PRAYER TO THE SAINTS:*

Ever-living God,
the signs of your love are manifest
in the honor you give your saints.
May their prayers and their example encour-
age us
to follow your Son more faithfully.
We ask this through Christ our Lord.

(Sacramentary, Common of Holy Men
and Women, 1.)

5. BYZANTINE PRAYER TO ALL-SAINTS:

O you apostles, martyrs, prophets, hierarchs,
righteous ones and holy women
who have fought the good fight and kept the
faith,
since you have acquired favor with the Savior,
we beseech you to intercede with him
in his goodness that he may save our souls.
O holy Mother, Mother of inexpressible Light,
we honor you with angelic hymns
and we all exalt with great devotion.
With the saints, O Lord,
grant rest to the souls of your servants,
where there is no pain, no sorrow, no sighing,
but everlasting life. Amen.

(Byzantine Rite, Ordinary, Saturdays.)

6. TO OUR GUARDIAN ANGEL:

Angel of God, my guardian dear,
to whom his love commits me here,
Ever this day (night) be at my side,
enlighten and guard, rule and guide me.
(Partial Indulgence, 8.)   *Amen.*

7. FOR THE SOULS IN PURGATORY:

Eternal rest, grant to them, O Lord,
and let perpetual light shine upon them.
May they rest in peace. Amen.

(Partial Indulgence, for the Poor Souls
only, 46.)

May it please you, O Lord,
to reward with eternal life all those

who do good for us for your Name's sake.
Amen.

(Partial Indulgence, 47.)

Note: A partial indulgence can be gained by praying the Opening Prayer from the Mass of a saint
or any approved prayer to the Saints.   54.

READING FOR PARALITURGIES
TO THE SAINTS

Lv. 19:1-2, 17-18.	Phil. 3:8-14.
Dt. 6:3-9.	Jas. 2:14-17.
1 Kings 19:4-9, 11-15.	1 Jn. 4:7-16.
Tb. 12:6-13.	
Pvr. 31:10-20.	Mt. 5:1-12.
Is. 58:6-11.	Mt. 5:13-16.
Zep. 2:3; 3:12-13.	Mt. 16:24-27.
1 Cor. 1:26-31.	Mt. 25:14-30.
1 Cor. 13:1-13.	Mk. 10:17-30.
Gal. 2:19-20.	Lk. 12:35-40.
Eph. 3:14-19.	Jn. 15:1-8.

Ps. 1:1-6
Ps. 15:2-5.
Ps. 34:2-11.
Ps. 103:1-8.
Ps. 112:1-9.

SANCTITY IS
THE LOVE OF GOD AND OF MEN
CARRIED TO
A SUBLIME EXTRAVAGANCE.

(Romano Guardini, 1885-)

9

NEWER FORMS OF DEVOTIONAL PARALITURGICAL PRAYER

Just before a meeting in another parish, a woman quietly came up to me and asked: "Father, have you accepted Jesus as your personal Savior?" When I assured her that I had, she confided in me that she was going to invite me to her prayer meeting if I had not. She said that her faith really began to make sense and that the Mass meant a whole lot more to her since she prayed in that intimate group.

It is rather interesting to find out that someone, who is very active in the parish liturgy and in parish or diocesan apostolic activities, also goes to a prayer group. In addition to all that the liturgy can and does mean to them, they still hunger for something more! This should not surprise us, since Pope Pius XII wrote of this possibility in his encyclical on the Liturgy in 1947. The II Vatican Council said about the same thing in its *Constitution on the Liturgy:* "The Liturgy does not exhaust the entire activity of the Church" (n. 9); and, "The spiritual life is not limited solely to participation in the Liturgy" (n. 12).

THE OLD AND THE NEW

Some people are returning to traditional forms of prayer and devotion, which have been updated in the light of the Council. Others are experimenting with some of the newer forms of prayer experiences which have appeared along with the Council. In their own way, each of these forms of prayer— traditional or modern—is challenging the person to grow in prayer, rather than settle on some intermediate plateau.

This call to better prayer is intimately tied up with one's growth in love and unity with God and neighbor. As one develops, so does the other. Hence, the Church offers us a wide variety of prayer experiences *in addition to and in subordination to the Liturgy*. This makes sense, since no form of prayer is the answer for everyone in the Church for all times. The Church reminds us of our need to pray alone and together, but she teaches that we have great freedom of choice outside of the Liturgy. At the same time, she carefully investigates these newer forms of prayer, allows their use, and sometimes promotes them for wider use in the Church.

Now that we have discussed the enduring value of popular devotions, let us turn our attention to some of these newer forms of prayer.

BIBLE DEVOTIONS

This form of prayer was urged by the Council, although it has been around much longer. Essentially, a Bible Devotion is like the first part of Mass, the Liturgy of the Word. The post-conciliar commission has been recommending the use of a short Liturgy of the Word with all the new sacramental rites, when the sacrament is not celebrated at Mass. (This is the case of Baptism, Confirmation, Marriage, Anointing, Reconciliation or Penance, Liturgies for Children, etc.) Besides this, the Church recommends various forms of the Liturgy of the Word by itself. This is more properly called the Bible Devotion.

Originally, the early Church added the synagogue service of the word to the brief service of "the breaking of the bread", which Christ asked his followers to celebrate "in memory of me". That synagogue service consisted of prayers, readings, and explanation, and a blessing. It was used in the villages and towns, whereas the sacred liturgy of the Old Testament was celebrated at the Temple in Jerusalem. Since the original Mass was very short, this was quite a natural addition. The Church used the Old Testament, and as she produced the epistles and Gospels, these were also used.

A Bible Devotion is a "paraliturgy"; that is, it exists along side of the liturgy. Sometimes it is non-eucharistic; sometimes it is eucharistic—when Benediction or a Communion Service is added to it.

The service usually starts with a hymn, followed by a scriptural greeting (like those used at the beginning of Mass). Then, the theme of the service is explained by a lector or the celebrant. Two or three bible readings follow, with a period of silent thought and prayer. A psalm or canticle from the Scriptures is used to respond to the reading.

Ordinarily, there is a homily or explanation. Other

prayers follow, especially prayers of the faithful. Sometimes, a common prayer or work of charity is suggested. (Benediction or Communion may follow the Service, but the service is complete without them as a Bible Devotion.)

Another variation of Bible Devotion is the Penitential Service. It involves many of the same elements, but they are aimed at helping the community become more aware of the communal nature of sin and reconciliation, and helping the people prepare for the Sacrament of Penance. The revised *Order of Penance* or Reconciliation offers some models of communal penance services. The individual confession can take place within such a service or apart from it.

(To encourage Bible reading, the Church offers a plenary indulgence for spending a half hour in this devout reading—under the usual conditions of Confession, Communion, and prayers for the Pope, 50.)

SHARED PRAYER

In the more recent history of spirituality, there is a partial turning away from the old concept of retiring away from others, to turn to God in prayer. While there will always be need for some intimate conversation with God *alone*, there is also the possibility of sharing in prayer.

"Shared prayer" in the past was usually a very structured prayer—often little more than praying at the same time as others with some very definite formulas. Such was the case with the Mass, the novena, Vespers, and so on.

The modern concept of shared prayer denotes a communal prayer, in which one prays out loud *at will* both to help and learn from the group at prayer. When one shares prayer, a passage of Scripture is read, a period of silence follows, and then, at one's own initiative, one shares an insight or offers a prayer generated from the reading.

Hymns and songs—other forms of prayer—are often added from time to time. Periods of silent thinking and prayer alternate—sometimes even vocal prayer. Mostly, though, shared prayer is in the words of the various individuals involved. Not everyone shares his prayers every time, and this is not noticed amid the spontaneous elements of shared prayer.

Some people feel uncomfortable with the idea of sharing prayer. This is natural, since their whole background was the "me and God" spirituality. One can not expect every temperament to like this form of prayer. Yet, many people brought up in the old style of praying have successfully adapted forms of shared prayer.

As a feeling of trust develops with the participants, many a person "opens up" in this new form of prayer. They later speak of a feeling of oneness before God and each other, a giving and receiving of strength from this community-in-Christ. Some admit that they continue in their old form of private prayer, while at the same time occasionally sharing prayer.

Shared prayer has some weaknesses as do all forms of prayer. Because it takes a certain "mood" or spirit of trust to share prayer with others, this prayer depends a lot on circumstances. Sometimes they are not favorable, and the sharing is strained or thin. Again, the prayer can turn from conversation with God to merely dialogue with one's neighbor. While anyone who has had some experience in sharing prayer could conduct a prayer service, a director should be sought to provide for long-range growth in prayer.

MEDITATION

Meditation has long been a part of the traditional prayer experience of the Church, but it is better known to priests and religious. The one new element in meditation, which is causing a bit of a stir, is that of seeking direction and technique from Eastern mysticism. In the far East, the holy men of past and present use special exercises called "yoga" to put themselves into a feeling of readiness for meditation. (Thomas Merton, the great Trappist, is a good author to consult on this matter.)

Interest in Eastern mysticism should not be construed as a rejection of nor a deficiency in Western mysticism. This would be unjust, since most people do not know enough about the two to compare them. The mysticism of the Catholic Church goes back to the hermits in the desert wastes of Egypt and the monasteries of Medieval Europe.

The spirituality of the Orthodox Churches and the Eastern Rites of the Catholic Church centers on the transcendence of God, while that of the Western

Rites focus on his immanence. Unfortunately, the monks had too great an influence on this spirituality; they did not help the laity produce one for their state in life. Since the days of St. Francis de Sales in the 17th Century, this lay spirituality has been gradually blooming.

Meditation can be described as attempting to enter into a wordless conversation with God. It seeks a deeper union with God through the processes of the soul, without reliance of prayer formulas. St. Francis de Sales explained it in this way in his *Treatise on the Love of God* (VI, 4):

"Every meditation is a thought, but every thought is not a meditation. We often have thoughts which have no aim or intention at all, but are simple musing...and however attentive this kind of thought may be, it cannot be called meditation. Sometimes we think attentively about something to understand its causes, effects, qualities; and this thinking is called study. But, when we think about the things of God, not to learn, but to kindle our love, that is called meditation." There you have it! Meditation is thinking of the things of God to kindle our love. The thinking is but a prelude to the affections of the soul for God.

There are many books available on the technique of meditating. It was the belief of some of the Saints and many spiritual writers that one had to learn how to meditate in a structured way in order to ready himself for the more spontaneous prayer of the experienced.

The market place is benefiting from the authors of contemporary books on prayer, who think that most anyone can come more quickly to this spontaneous prayer. Besides those books which look like blank verse and photo-inspired meditation, much serious effort has been made in this direction. In the final analysis, one will have to judge the validity of structured or non-structured meditation by how well it helps one to lovingly unite his or her heart to God, bring forth affection, and then live a life of union with God and others.

Since one does not need much technique for non-structured meditation, a few words ought to be said about the other kind. One can investigate the Catholic tradition on meditation in the *Spiritual Exercises* of St. Ignatius Loyola or in the *Introduction to the Devout Life* by St. Francis de Sales. They should be available at one's public library or from better Catholic book stores in paperback form.

To meditate properly, you must prepare for it. You must read a few thoughts or "points" for meditation. Then you must set aside a definite time for it, in a place conducive to prayer.

The first step in the actual meditation is clearing the mind of its usual preoccupations and then placing oneself in the presence of God. Then begin to consider the "points" of meditation. The goal is to pass from thinking to praying in wordless conversation with God. This dialogue should involve both listening and speaking.

As the meditation matures, the thoughts are replaced with affections of love, gratitude, humility, awe, and so on. The meditation is often concluded with a resolution to carry out what one has thought about. Often, a vocal prayer, which expresses a similar thought or affection, concludes the period of meditation.

A formal technique of meditation is often useful for a beginner. He needs the discipline of the method to learn to set aside time for it, as well as make the proper preparations for fruitful prayer. The contemporary books on non-structured meditation remind one of St. Teresa of Avila's description of meditative recitation of prayers and meditative reading. She advised them as alternate methods to her more formal way of meditating. Even the use of a meaningful word or phrase over and over again (a mantra) is also mentioned by her as a meditative recitation of a prayer.

Like all forms of prayer, meditation has its weaknesses.

The first is to turn meditation into a refined process of study. But, meditation is not thinking so much as effective praying.

Another danger is to think that other forms of prayer and spiritual reading can now be done away with. Just as a well which is not continually filled with water from some source will run dry, so will meditation unless it is fueled with prayer and study.

Meditation has many degrees and one can fail to move on to a more mature form of prayer. After one has mastered meditation, there is acquired contemplation. In this form of prayer, the action of man is getting smaller and that of God greater. If God so wills, one can even pass on to higher degrees of contemplation, which is God's gift to the person.

Contemplation is a prayer of great simplicity, less conscious effort, and much love and union with God. Because there are so many degrees of proficiency in both meditation and contemplation, the services of an experienced spiritual director are essential. For his part, the director must have the time, inclination, knowledge and experience to lead one into these higher types of prayer.

Meditation is not incompatible with other forms of prayer. The Saints regularly engaged in mental prayer, joined in the liturgical prayer of their community, and offered other forms of prayer. One could see how shared prayer could also be part of this regime of prayer.

There are so many meditation books on the market—both reissues of classics and newly written, that you should find little trouble in this regard. Since every priest and religious has training and experience in meditating, there is ample advice available. You have only to put your mind to it, find the time and place, and begin to meditate.

CHARISMATIC PRAYER

There are tens of thousands of American Catholics who are discovering another form of prayer called pentecostal or charismatic prayer. St. Paul spoke of unique gifts of the Holy Spirit in several of his epistles—especially in 1 Corinthians 12, 13, and 14. While the Church has acknowledged these gifts throughout her long history in certain individuals, many modern Christians claim that these gifts are more common than usually thought. In the Protestant tradition, pentecostals have regularly been present; now one finds them in the Catholic Church.

Pentecostal or charismatic prayer is another form of communal prayer, in which the activities of the Holy Spirit are sought and observed. The Holy Spirit, obviously, is continually at work in the Church and in the individual, helping everyone to grow in holiness and in love. While many people are not consciously attuned to these workings of the Spirit, one can accustom himself or herself to notice this influence.

Charismatic prayer also offers God much conscious praise. While many other Christians rely heavily on prayers of petition, the charismatic first directs his attention to praising and thanking God. A favorite phrase of these Christians is: "Praise the Lord". (Praise is not absent from liturgical prayer, since the Church bids us praise God with the "Glory to God in the Highest", the "Holy, Holy, Holy", the concluding lines of the Eucharistic Prayers, and so on.)

Finally, the charismatic recognizes the presence of special gifts of the Holy Spirit in the world today. Many of their members claim the gifts of wisdom, power to express knowledge, faith, healing, miraculous powers, prophecy, distinguishing spirits, speaking in tongues, and so on. (St. Paul explains these gifts in Romans 12: 6-8, 1 Corinthians 12: 8-11; Ephesians 4: 11, etc.) Charismatics do not claim unusual amounts of *natural* gifts, but rather the possession of *supernatural* gifts of the Holy Spirit, destined to build up the Church.

The Catholic Church cautiously teaches that this is quite possible. In actual practice, though, the

Church has often recognized their presence only *after* the event. For example, Pope John XXIII was well within his authority to call together an Ecumenical Council. But, the good pope said that he called it under an "inspiration". Now, in the light of the early fruits of this far-reaching Council, the Church judges that this inspiration was not just and ordinary grace from God but an inspiration of the Holy Spirit.

Many charismatic prayer meetings follow a general pattern. First there is a hymn to get people in a prayerful mood. This is followed by a reading from Scripture. A period of silent thought and prayer follows. Praise is offered to God. Some prayer is shared. Another song may follow then or later. Several people might witness to the action of the Holy Spirit in their own lives or in the community. This in turn gives rise to more praise and thanksgiving.

This joyous prayer is occasionally augmented by someone "speaking in tongues". The actual words used sound unintelligible, but the individual involved knows that he or she is offering praise to the Lord. This may or may not be followed by an interpretation, given by another gifted person. This interpretation often takes the form of a free quotation from the Bible. Occasionally, hands are laid on the sick to seek a cure, or to bring about the "Baptism of the Spirit".

Since Christ spoke of baptism "in water and Spirit" (John 3,5), charismatics hold to a unique experience of the Spirit which may accompany but often follows the Sacraments of Baptism and Confirmation. This experience accompanies a more definitive conversion or a more conscious dedication to God's work. The prayer meeting produces a warm feeling of fellowship and the presence of God. Since the service follows its own rhythm and pattern, many people appreciate it as an *addition to* the more structured form of liturgical prayer.

The person, who might like to try charismatic prayer, should first read the First Letter of St. Paul to the Corinthians, in which he explains the origin of these gifts, their purpose of building up the Church, the need of great practical charity in the lives of all, the gifts of prophecy and tongues in great detail, and the rules of order to be followed at prayer meetings. (Read all of chapters 12 to 14 in this epistle.)

The *Constitution on the Church* (chapter II, n. 12) clearly states that the Church herself is a charismatic community, continually under the influence of the Holy Spirit, who recreates and directs her through ordinary and special gifts or charisms. The Church teaches that these gifts or charisms are given at will by the Holy Spirit to whomsoever he wishes for building up and reforming the Church.

Since the days of the *Acts of the Apostles*—with its fifty-two references to the Spirit's activity on the early Church—the Church sees this activity in both the *commissioned ministries* such as bishops, as well as *others freely chosen by the Spirit*. This means that the Holy Spirit directs the Church through appointed channels and in other ways too. Sometimes this may produce tension, when the Spirit calls for reform or growth in addition to those initiated by persons with the charism of office.

The years which have followed upon the Council

have seen this tension. The hierarchy has been very busy carrying out the reforms of the Council, and other influences have also been at work in the Church. Some have been of God, and others of men.

The latter are indicated by the temptation to rebel against legitimate authority acting within its competence, the preference of personal will as opposed to the community good, the presence of pride and illusion, the breaking down rather than the building up of the Church, and so on. But, not all tension should be ascribed to these deficiencies. Much of it is the tension of growing pains, as the old matures even more or gives way to the new.

Charismatic prayer has its weaknesses. Some people are so attracted to it, that they give up other necessary forms of prayer, including the liturgy. Others show a tendency to religious and biblical fundamentalism—overlooking even the most solid gains of modern biblical and theological scholarship.

Sometimes it produces a simplistic attitude towards life in which some of the ordinary struggle and planning, which God expects of the being he has endowed with intelligence and grace, is turned back to God for completion. Others are so attracted to the special gifts, especially of tongues, that they grade religious people by their possession or lack of these gifts.

Charismatics may show signs of theological and ecumenical confusion. This latter often appears in mixed or ecumenical prayer groups. Deep-seated theological or ecclesiastical problems, which have separated Christians for centuries are not settled by simply ignoring them or working out oversimplified solutions. These problems must be worked out with head and heart, with full commitment to the years of effort which will be needed to solve them. While one should be encouraged and appreciate that Christians are worshipping together, this is best done with common elements rather than in areas which offer in principle no easy solution.

For the Catholic pentecostal or charismatic, the teaching authority of the Church will always be his safeguard. It is obvious that the Holy Spirit working with those with the charism of office will not be in contradiction to himself working in those to whom he gives other special gifts.

A clear sign that one has the Spirit of Christ, the Paraclete, is that he or she takes part in the Mass and sacraments regularly, follows the teaching authority of the Church, and works with those who have the charism of office through the regular activities of the parish, community and diocese. In a very real sense, the charismatic and other prayer activities will be in addition to and not a substitution for liturgical and other forms of community prayer. (An additional safeguard for the Catholic charismatic is a leadership group strongly influenced by a theologian and spiritual director. This person should have experience particularly in "discernment of spirits", since the danger of delusion and pride are great.)

Charismatic prayer is not for everyone. Because it is very new to many people, it should be sympathetically and honestly evaluated. *In all of these newer forms of prayer*, one should possess a great openness and prudence. One can but investigate these matters carefully, seek the advice of an experienced and open spiritual guide—sometimes several if the matter is new even to them, and cautiously put one's heart and soul into the matter.

If it is of God, then it will lead us to an even greater degree of prayer, love, union and service. If the result of the experience is division into our own special little groups, at real variance with the Church and its teaching, and without much visible service to our fellowmen, then it can hardly be of God.

One should always remember that practically every division from the Mystical Body was started by those who thought that they were so right, but inwardly were influenced by some human error, pride or illusion. The words of St. Paul to the Ephesians must always be our yardstick:

"Make an effort to preserve the unity which has the Spirit as its origin and peace as its binding force. There is but one body, and one Spirit, just as there is but one hope given all of you by your call. There is one Lord, one faith, one baptism, one God and Father of all, who is over all, and works through all, and is in all" (Ephesians 4: 3-6).

PRAYERS TO THE HOLY SPIRIT

1. *LITURGICAL PRAYER TO THE HOLY SPIRIT:*

*Father of light, from whom every good
     gift comes,
send your Spirit into our lives
with the power of a mighty wind,
and by the flame of your wisdom
open the horizons of our minds.
Loosen our tongues to sing your praise
in words beyond the power of speech,
for without your Spirit
man could never raise his voice in words
     of peace
or announce the truth that Jesus is Lord,
who lives and reigns with you and
     the Holy Spirit,
one God, for ever and ever.*

(Sacramentary, Alternate Prayer, Pentecost.)

2. TRADITIONAL PRAYER TO THE HOLY SPIRIT:

Come, Holy Spirit,
fill the hearts of your faithful
and enkindle in them
the fire of your love.
(Partial indulgence, 62.)

3. EASTERN RITE PRAYER TO THE HOLY SPIRIT:

Cast me not afar from your face, and let your guiding Spirit dwell in me. Heavenly King, Consoler, the Spirit of Truth, present in all places and filling all things, the Treasury of Blessings and the Gift of Life: come and dwell in us, cleanse us of all stain, and save our souls. O Good One! Glory be to the Father and to the Son and to the Holy Spirit, now and always and for ever and ever. Amen.
O Holy Consoler, save us who sing to you. Alleluia.

(Byzantine Rite, Office of Pentecost.)

4. ANOTHER TRADITIONAL PRAYER:

O Holy Spirit, divine Spirit of light and love, I consecrate to you my understanding, my heart and my will, my whole being for time and eternity. May my understanding be always submissive to your heavenly inspirations and to the teachings of the holy Catholic Church, of

which you are the infallible Guide; may my
heart be ever inflamed with love of God and
of my neighbor; may my will be ever conformed
to the divine will, and may my whole life be
a faithful imitation of the life and virtues of
Our Lord and Savior Jesus Christ, to whom
with the Father and you be honor and glory
for ever.   Amen.

(The Raccolta,   289.)

5.   PRAYER FOR CHRIST'S SPIRIT

O Lord Jesus Christ, give us
such a measure of your Spirit that we may be
enabled
to obey your teaching: to pacify anger, to take
part in pity,
to moderate desire, to increase love,
to put away sorrow, to cast away vain-glory;
not to be vindictive, not to fear death;
ever entrusting our spirit to the immortal God
who with you and the Holy Spirit lives
and reigns world without end.   Amen.

(St. Appolonius.)

READINGS FOR PARALITURGIES TO THE SPIRIT

Is. 11: 1-4.

Is. 42: 1-3.

Is. 61: 1-9.

Jl. 2: 23; 3: 1-3.

Ez. 36: 24-28.

Acts. 2: 1-6.

Acts. 8: 1-4, 14-17.

Acts. 19: 1-6.

Rom. 8: 14-17.

Rom. 8: 26-27.

1 Cor. 12: 4-13.

Eph. 1: 3-4, 13-19.

Mk. 1: 9-11.

Lk. 4: 16-22.

Lk. 10: 21-24.

Jn. 7: 37-39.

Jn. 14: 15-17.

Jn. 15: 18-21; 26-27.

Jn. 16: 5-7, 12-13.

Ps. 22: 23-32.

Ps. 96: 1-12.

Ps. 104: 24-34.

Ps. 145: 2-11.

MEDITATION IS THE SOURCE
OF LOVE
AND OF APOSTOLIC DRIVE
FOR GREAT
AND GENEROUS ACTIONS.

(St. Teresa of Avila, 1515-1582.)

10

VARIOUS
NEEDS

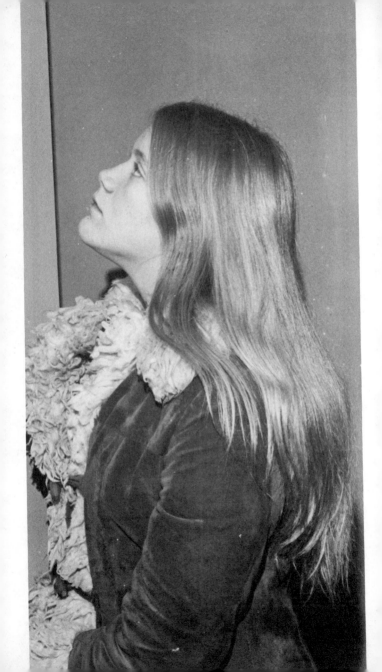

PRAYERS FOR VARIOUS OCCASIONS

THRICE HOLY PRAYER

Holy is God! Holy Mighty One! Holy the Immortal One! Have mercy on us. (Three times.)

Glory be to the Father and to the Son and to the Holy Spirit, now and always and for ever and ever.

Holy the Immortal One! Have mercy on us! Holy is God! Holy the Mighty One! Holy the Immortal One! Have mercy on us.

(Common to almost all the Eastern Rite Churches.)

THE JESUS PRAYER

LORD, HAVE MERCY,
LORD JESUS, HAVE MERCY ON ME A SINNER.

The phrase, "Have mercy" in the Western Rite is often a plea for forgiveness. In the Eastern Rites, it is a general prayer for all that man should say to God and about him: it asks divine mercy; it acknowledges God's greatness and goodness. It is made on behalf of the cosmos—inanimate, human and angelic; it is a cry of love; it is an act of dedication; it is the opening of one's being to God and so on. That is why it is repeated often—sometimes thirty, forty and fifty times. It is the word of love, always repeated, always new; LORD, HAVE MERCY.

AN ACT OF FAITH, HOPE, LOVE AND SORROW

My God, I believe in You, I hope in You, I love You above all things with all my soul, with all my heart and with all my strength. I love you because you are infinitely good and worthy of being loved; and because I love you, I repent with all my heart for having offended you. Have mercy on me, a sinner. Amen.

(Partial Indulgence,   2; The Raccolta,   37.)

PRAYER FOR SERENITY AND WISDOM

O God, grant me the serenity to accept
the things that I cannot change,
the courage to change the things I can,
and the wisdom to know the difference.

(Reinhold Niebuhr, 1892-1971.)

MOTHER MARY STEWARD'S PRAYER

Keep us, O Lord, from all pettiness.
Let us be large in thought, in word, in deed.
Let us be done with fault-finding
and leave off all self-seeking.

May we put away all pretense,
and meet each other face-to-face,
without self-seeking and without prejudice.
May we never be hasty in judgment,
and always be generous.
Let us take time for all things,
and make us grow calm, serene, and gentle.
Teach us to put into action our better impulses,
to be straightforward and unafraid.
Grant that we may realize that
it is the little things of life that create differences.

THANKS FOR SPECIAL MOMENTS OF GRACE

We give thee thanks, O God, for the great moments of joy and strength that come to us when by a strong and special movement of grace we are able to perform some act of pure and disinterested love. For the clean fire of that love which floods the soul and cleanses the whole man and leaves us filled with an unexpected lightness and freedom for action. For the moment of pure prayer which not only establishes order in the soul, but even fortifies us against physical weariness and brings us a new lease on life itself. Glory be to thee for thy previous gift!

(Thomas Merton, 1915-1968.)

PRAYER IN SPIRITUAL DISCOURAGEMENT

My Jesus, banish the demon of discouragement. My devotion has vanished; my fervor seems to be at low ebb; spiritual thoughts no longer soothe my troubled soul. Even the remembrances of Thy passion and of Thy Blessed Mother grow dim before my vision. O Jesus, do not forsake me. Help me! I am resolved not to omit a single one of my devotions. Hear me, O my God, strengthen and increase my faith. Keep me from yielding to temptation. Thou hast said, "My yoke is sweet; my burden light." Have mercy on me, for wheresoever I turn I see naught but obstacles and difficulties. Were my faith strong I would thank Thee for my trials; but, alas, I feel only impatience, doubt, and discouragement. Do Thou, my soul, hold fast to Jesus. How fainthearted and childish I am! All my comfort, all my joy must come from Thee. Receive me again into Thy favor. If it be Thy Will that these temptations assail me, I beseech Thee, suffer me not to fall. O Lord, my God, I cast myself entirely into Thy hands. Worn out by the struggle I will rest beneath Thy Cross. I embrace it. O Mother Mary, pray for me, a poor sinner; pray for me in my great desolation of soul. Jesus, be merciful to me. Amen.

(St. John Neumann, 1811-1859.)

PRAYER FOR THE SANCTIFICATION OF LIFE
(This prayer can be a responsive prayer.)

Help us, save us, have mercy on us and protect us, O God, by your grace. Lord, have mercy.

That this whole day may be perfect, holy, peaceful, and without sin, let us ask the Lord. Grant this, O Lord.

For an angel of peace, a faithful guide and guardian of our souls and bodies, let us ask the Lord. Grant this, O Lord.

For the forgiveness and remission of our sins and offenses, let us ask the Lord. Grant this, O Lord.

For what is good and profitable to our souls and for peace in the world, let us ask the Lord. Grant this, O Lord.

That the rest of our life may be spent in peace and repentance, let us ask the Lord. Grant this, O Lord.

That the end of our life may be Christian, painless, unashamed and peaceful, and for a good defense before the awesome judgment seat of Christ, let us ask the Lord. Grant this, O Lord.

Let us remember our all-holy, spotless, most highly blessed and glorious Lady, the Mother of God and ever-virgin Mary, with all the saints, and commend ourselves and one another and our whole life to Christ God. To you, O Lord we pray.

(Common to many Eastern Rites)

PRAYER FOR ALL MEN

O most holy Heart of Jesus, shower your blessings on all men and women, because they are my brothers and sisters in you. Bless your Church, the Pope, all bishops, priests, deacons, religious, seminarians, and candidates to the dedicated state.

To the just grant perseverance. Convert sinners. Bless our relatives, friends, and benefactors. Strengthen missionaries and increase vocations. Aid the physically and mentally ill. Help the aging and dying. Deliver the holy souls from Purgatory. And extend over all hearts the merciful empire of your love. AMEN.

PRAYER IN THE NAME OF ALL MEN

Jesus, Lover of mankind, although you came centuries ago to be the way, the truth, and the life, countless men and women do not know you, do not love you as they could, and are even indifferent to you. I offer you all the good which everyone has done, but especially the good which is not consciously offered to you, my Lord. May you be honored and loved in some way by them too. AMEN.

PRAYER FOR MY PARENTS

My God, I thank you for the sacrament of Matrimony, which provided me with a Catholic home. Bless my dear parents who have cooperated with your graces and have taken care of me. Bless them for the Catholic education they have provided for me. Bless them for the good example they have given me. Bless them for the prayers they have taught me. Bless them for the corrections they have given me. Bless them for the home training I have received at their hands. Bless them for all the prayers they have said for me. Bless them for the encouragement which they gave me in my selection of a vocation. Grant them your comforts in this life; grant them a happy death, and then eternal glory in heaven. May I by my life be an honor to them by serving you, your Church, my loved ones, and my neighbors. AMEN.

PRAYER FOR MY FAMILY

Almighty and loving Father, in your goodness,

you have led me and my (wife, husband) to be united in human love and in the Sacrament of Matrimony. You share with us your power to give life and to be signs of love and unity in the world —after the model of Christ's loving union with the Church. Help us to make our home a domestic church, where prayer, love, peace, purity, faith and happiness will be lived and respected. Be with us in our moments of joy and strengthen us in our hour of trial. Aid us especially when our children cause us worries, and when it is difficult to make ends meet. Help us to grow in wisdom, age and grace as we fulfill our responsibilities and mature ever in love. We ask this through Christ our Lord. AMEN.

PRAYER FOR FRIENDS AND RELATIVES

O blessed Lord, you have commanded us to love one another, so we pray you to grant us the grace to love everyone in you and for you. We ask your mercy for all, but especially for the relatives and friends whom your love has given us. Love them, O fountain of love, and make them love you with all their hearts, that they may will, and speak, and do those things only which are pleasing to you. AMEN.

(St. Anselm, 1033-1109.)

PRAYER FOR MYSELF

O most holy Heart of Jesus, fountain of all good, I adore you, I love you, and, being deeply sorry for my sins, I offer you this heart of mine. Make it

237

humble, patient, pure, and completely conformed to yours. Grant, good Jesus, that I may live in and for you. Protect me in all dangers; console me in my afflictions; give me health of body, assistance in my temporal needs, your blessings on all my undertakings, and the grace of a happy death. AMEN.

(The Raccolta, 263.)

PRAYER FOR PRIESTS AND RELIGIOUS LEADERS

O Jesus, eternal High Priest, who in an incomparable act of love for men, your brothers, willed that the priesthood should proceed from your Sacred Heart. O Jesus, strengthen your priests for their difficult vocation. Live in them; transform them into yourself; make them instruments of your mercy; act in them and through them; re-live in them in very truth; and once again traverse the world teaching, pardoning, consoling, sacrificing, renewing the sacred bond of Love between the Heart of God and the hearts of men.

Bless also all the Christian priests, ministers, rabbis, and other religious leaders of the world, who are instruments in some way of your love and mercy. Bless their labors and may the souls to whom they minister be their joy and consolation here and their everlasting crown. AMEN.

PRAYER DURING A JOURNEY

Jesus cum Maria, Sit nobis in via.
Jesus with Mary, Be with us on our way.

(Christopher Columbus, 1451-1506.)

LEAD, KINDLY LIGHT

Lead, kindly Light, amid the encircling gloom,
    Lead thou me on!
The night is dark, and I am far from home,
    Lead thou me on!
Keep thou my feet; I do not ask to see
The distant scene,—one step is enough for me.
I was not ever thus, nor prayed that thou
Shouldst lead me on.
I loved to see and choose my path, but now
    Lead thou me on!
I loved the garish day, and, spite of fears,
Pride ruled my will; remember not past years;
So long thy power hath blest me, sure it **still**
    Will lead me on
O'er moor and fen, o'er crag and torrent, till
    The night is gone;
And with the morn those angel faces smile,
While I have loved long since, and lost awhile.

(Henry Cardinal Newman, 1801-1890.)

IN ANY SPECIAL NEED

Say not, merciful Virgin, that you cannot help me; for your beloved Son has given you all power in heaven and on earth. Say not that you ought not to assist me, for you are the Mother of all the poor children of Adam, and mine in particular. Since then, merciful Virgin, you are my Mother and you are all-powerful, what excuse can you offer if you do not lend your assistance? See, my Mother, see, you are obliged to grant me what I ask, and to yield to my entreaties.

(St. Francis de Sales, 1567-1622.)

PRAYER FOR THE MISSIONS

Lord Jesus, Lover of mankind, it was you who sent forth your apostles and all their helpers so many centuries ago to preach the Gospel and make disciples of all the nations. Even now, though, countless billions do not know you and many are even indifferent to you. I humbly pray that you be with your missionaries everywhere, as they continue to carry on the task you gave so long ago. Sanctify all missionaries, and inspire all Christians to support them in prayer and in other ways. Help them to be respectful of that part of good which is in other religions, even as they share the Gospel with them. Strengthen them in their many works of charity, and in their efforts to share the riches of the Church, Mass, Sacraments, and your other blessings with all peoples. Build up, especially, the native clergy, convert sinners, and offer all men the grace to know and love you, their Savior and Brother. We ask this in faith and in your name. AMEN.

FOR UNITY OF CHRISTIANS

Lord, lover of mankind, fill us with the love your Spirit gives. Hear the prayers of your people and bring the hearts of all believers together in your praise and in common sorrow for sins. Heal all divisions among Christians that we may rejoice in the perfect unity of your Church and move together as one to eternal life in your kingdom. Grant this through our Lord Jesus Christ, your Son, who lives

240

and reigns with you and the Holy Spirit, one God, for ever and ever. AMEN.

(Adapted from the Sacramentary.)

ARMENIAN LITURGICAL PRAYER

Blessed are you, O Holy Father, true God. AMEN.
Blessed are you, O Holy Son, true God. AMEN.
Blessed are you, O Holy Spirit, true God. AMEN.

Praise and honor be to the Father and Son and Holy Spirit now and always from eternity to eternity. AMEN.

Look down upon us, O Lord Jesus Christ, from heaven, from your holy place, and from the glorious throne of your Kingdom; come to sanctify us and give us life, you who are enthroned with the Father, and offered here; please make us, and through the ministry of your priest, all this people, partakers of your spotless Body and of your precious Blood.

(Armenian Rite.)

THE CHIEF EXERCISE OF PRAYER
IS TO SPEAK TO GOD
AND TO HEAR GOD SPEAK
IN THE BOTTOM OF YOUR HEART.

(St. Francis de Sales, 1567-1622.)

241

BIBLIOGRAPHY

Abeyasungha, N., *Devotions Today, Priest Magazine* (June, 1973), pp. 35-37.

Behold Your Mother, Woman of Faith, (Washington: Publications Office, United States Catholic Conference, 1974).

Bouyer, Louis, *Life and Liturgy,* (New York: Sheed and Ward, 1956), pp. 243-256.

Braso, Gabriel, *Liturgy and Spirituality,* (Collegeville: The Liturgical Press, 1962), pp. 189-204.

Dehne, Carl, *Roman Catholic Popular Devotions, Worship Magazine,* (October, 1975), pp. 446-460.

Holy Communion and Worship of the Eucharist Outside Mass, (Washington: Publications Office, United States Catholic Conference, 1974).

Howell, Clifford, *Of Sacraments and Sacrifice,* (Collegeville: The Liturgical Press. pp. 153-163.

Jungmann, Josef, *The Good News Yesterday and Today,* (New York: Sadlier, 1962), pp. 132-150.

Jungmann, Josef, *Announcing the Good News,* (New York: Herder and Herder, 1967), pp. 86-89.

Jungmann, Josef, *The Mass,* (Collegeville: The Liturgical Press, 1975).

Koser, Constance, *Liturgy and Popular Devotions* in Liturgy of Vatican II (Chicago: Franciscan Herald Press).

Nelson, John, *Today's Ecology of Devotion, Worship Magazine,* (Dec. 1965), pp. 649-659.

O'Shea, William, *The Worship of the Church,* (Westminster: The Newman Press, 1958), pp. 545-558.

Paul VI, *Marian Devotions* (Washington, Publications Office, United States Catholic Conference, 1974).

Schutte, Grace, *Reflections on Prayer and Worldly Holiness, Worship Magazine* (February, 1967), pp. 105-114.

Sheet, J., *Personal and Liturgical Prayer: Responses to Christ's Paschal Presence, Worship Magazine,* (August-September, 1973), pp. 412-416.

INDEX

ALBA BOOKS

**THE JESUS EXPERIENCE by Edward Car-
ter, S.J. — The "institutional" Church
may be in difficulties, but its Founder,
Jesus, is riding the crest of a new wave
of popularity. In this age, avid for
"experiences," Fr. Carter writes mov-
ingly of the one experience which produces permanent effects: meeting Jesus.**

$1.75

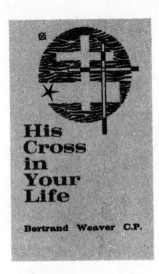

His
Cross
in
Your
Life

Bertrand Weaver C.P.

HIS CROSS IN YOUR LIFE by Bertrand Weaver, C.P. — It is said that too much concentration on the Cross produces a distorted Christianity — Easter, after all, is the center of our religion, not Calvary.

This may be so but, however strongly you believe in future felicity, for the most part you have to live with present pain. Suffering is a fact of life for all of us and nobody can escape the great decision: live, suffer and die like a Christian, or live, suffer and die like a dog.

This is not a new book — indeed the author is long since dead — but its theme is as relevant now as it was when he wrote it and as it will be a thousand years hence. Instead of consideration of THE Passion it offers practical help with YOUR Passion — what to do when the hand of the Lord touches your life. Its clear and concise prose is a joy to read.

$1.75

serafino falvo

THE HOUR OF THE HOLY SPIRIT

THE HOUR OF THE HOLY SPIRIT by Sera-fino Falvo — The Charismatic Movement continues to spread. This book is a revelation: testimony piles on testimony of the radical changes people have experienced in their lives. It is an ex-cellent presentation of the Charismatic Movement and will encourage many to go deeper into the life of the Spirit.

— **$3.30**

ALBA BOOKS

1.65

Keep Your OLD FOLKS At Home

KEEP YOUR OLD FOLKS AT HOME. By Theresa Bucchieri. Alba House, Canfield, Ohio, 1975. Pp. xii, 175. Paper, $1.65.

Now is the time for such a book! It is a true-to-life experience by the author, who is still to this date caring for a ninety-year-old senile aunt. Theresa Bucchieri has traveled abroad for the research so thoroughly expounded in this work, so badly needed by a society who looks upon the golden years as an evil to be done away with. Who are we to say how long we shall live?

The foreword is written by a local judge, Lisa Aversa Richette, and gives ample food for thought to those of us whose apostolate consists of visiting the aged in all types of institutions and in their homes, where they live alone and die alone, unloved, unwanted and uncared for. Throughout the author's long tenure in the U.S. Labor Department's Wage and Hour Division she has helped enforce the Fair Labor Standards Act for handicapped workers and aged at special minimum wages.

The author's style makes delightful reading and is an inspiration to all.

Sister Pasqualina Mazzatenta, M.P.F.
Saint Mary's of the Lake Convent
Watkins Glen, New York

"SISTERS TODAY" **MAY 1976**

An Interesting Thought

The publication you have just finished reading is part of the apostolic efforts of the Society of St. Paul of the American Province. A small, unique group of priests and brothers, the members of the Society of St. Paul propose to bring the message of Christ to men through the communications media while living the religious life.

If you know a young man who might be interested in learning more about our life and mission, ask him to contact the Vocation Office in care of the Society of St. Paul, Alba House Community, Canfield, Ohio 44406 (phone 216/533-5503). Full information will be sent without cost or obligation. You may be instrumental in helping a young man to find his vocation in life.

An interesting thought.